IN THE NAME OF EDITORIAL FREEDOM

IN THE NAME OF EDITORIAL FREEDOM

125 Years at the *Michigan Daily*

Edited and with an Introduction by
STEPHANIE STEINBERG

University of Michigan Press
ANN ARBOR

Published in the United States of America by
The University of Michigan Press
Manufactured in the United States of America
⊚ Printed on acid-free paper

2018   2017   2016   2015   4   3   2   1

A CIP catalog record for this book is available from the British Library.
ISBN 978-0-472-03637-0 (paper)
ISBN 978-0-472-12122-9 (e-book)

For every journalist who once called 420 Maynard home.

CONTENTS

FOREWORD

TOM HAYDEN

Around Maynard, young *Michigan Daily* staffers sometimes call us "the ghosts," the old *Daily* alumni who come wandering up the stairs with vacant looks just to remember the place. No doubt the intense 24/7 *Daily* experience leaves an indelible impression on the lives of those "ghosts." But it is more than nostalgia. Compared to the menu of other options in University of Michigan life, the *Daily* has a way of accelerating the process of "growing up" and at the same time making an actual difference in the University for years to come.

The importance of this *Daily* experience at its best will grow as technology and monopolistic capitalism progress. According to the *New York Times*, there now are more campus newspapers than all daily newspapers in the United States, about 1,800 to a declining 1,380.[1] College papers appear to be a greater source of local print news for American readers than the local papers they have long depended on. The *Daily*, one of the foremost campus papers, has outlasted its old competitor, the *Ann Arbor News*, which succumbed as a daily paper in 2009.

These facts matter. As a single example, it was the *Daily* that uncovered a 2009 sexual assault involving a top Michigan football player whom the University failed to take action against until his place-kicking career was over four years later. Thanks to the *Daily*'s coverage, the U.S. Department of Education's Office for Civil Rights is investigating the University's role in the possible cover-up. This is controversial stuff for young people to

---

1. The *New York Times*, April 13, 2014. In 1965, there were 1,751 daily newspapers in the United States, according to American Newspaper Publishers Association.

take on; I doubt that the alumni are surrounding Maynard and chanting "Go Blue!"

Readers, can you remember what the pressure is like when you are eighteen to twenty-one years old, sweating a deadline, fearing a mistake, calculating the consequences of crossing swords with the administrators who may drop the hammer on you for disturbing the reputation and financial resources of the University? There was a time decades ago when in loco parentis—the power of the University to act as a substitute parent—was the legal consensus, and when freedom of the campus press was hardly guaranteed. Echoes of in loco parentis still remain in our culture.

We who lived, breathed, and sometimes slept at the *Daily* went through an educational process that tested us, that mattered, that would remain forever in our bones. In those times, it was common to define the four years of higher education as a "parenthesis" in real life, a bubble free of any risks and consequences, a preparatory period of adulthood, which somehow would occur immediately after graduation. In a similar way, students were encouraged to acquire knowledge at a distance, by rote, objectively, without immersion or subjectivity. Neither as students nor as reporters were we allowed to permit the intrusion of feelings in our pristine observations.

At the *Daily*, all this was turned upside down. It is true, we were rookies in publishing an everyday newspaper, improvising and learning as we were doing it, in the spirit of John Dewey, one of the philosophical inspirers of participatory democracy, who preached of learning by doing. But that was the point. The collective practice of publishing the paper, from assigning stories in the morning to seeing the copies roll off the large web press by 3:00 a.m., was one requiring investigation, collaboration, choices, priorities, communication skills, meeting deadlines under pressure, and constant feedback from the University community, not just a professor behind a desk. A "B-minus" effort at the *Daily* wasn't acceptable, although it was a passing grade in class. Of course we did foolish things—I remember as a freshman being assigned to write editorials on subjects I knew nothing about. Mine was on the Baghdad Pact (I was opposed). If these were trial runs of our alacrity, there should have been warning labels (perhaps "test editorial") for *Daily* readers.

This *Daily* experience may have been unique in its raw intensity, but was paralleled throughout undergraduate life in ways that our parents and professors did not experience. For example, the dean of women in 1960–61 operated a network of dormitory advisors, known as "den mothers," who monitored coeds' personal behavior, sending letters to parents when a white woman was seen in social company of a black man. One of my undergraduate friends, Shirley Davis, wrote this poem in response:

Epistle to Dean Bacon upon Being Denied
Apartment Permission

With due respect to your temporal pow'r,
Most undergrad coeds before you cow'r
We realize that we're in your gracious care,
And thank thee nightly for our rooms so bare,
Our homey rooms of cheerful grey and brown,
With closet—if you look—and bed of down.
But ah! Let's not complain—we have the joys
Of community life minus the boys!
For this above all, we thank you Dear Dean,
It keeps our minds and morals clean!
All people as old and wise as you are
Know that young girls who can't get served in a bar
Are, as well, too young to live on their own,
Even if armed with "yes" letters from home!
Unsupervised housing! Ye Gods—what sin.
No hours, no rules, no house "moms" to come in
To see that by twelve we're sober in state,
To look under beds to check for a date.
Who knows what gross things by young girls be done,
If allowed freedom before twenty-one!
I'm with you Good Dean, I realize your plight.
I just want to ask you if one thing's all right—
Mind—I accept your ultimatum
(I'm trained to submit to rules, though I hate'm.)
But if, before age, I should wed some young male,
Would you let me out of this god-damned jail?

That's the way we were. We lived in the dull silence after McCarthyism, during the dawn of the counterculture, civil rights, the ban-the-bomb movement, and student activism. We knew nothing of investigative journalism, but it was made to sound vaguely inappropriate. Yet the very nature of publishing the *Daily* every day caused us to engage and form opinions, however tentatively. The vestiges of adolescence quickly faded as tests of maturity became everyday experiences:

> In 1959, a "deep throat" student encouraged me to write a seven-part series exposing racial and religious bans on membership in Acacia, Alpha Tau Omega, Sigma Chi, and Sigma Nu. The issue was exploding across the country. The University was preaching gradual change through education. It caused me to reject initiation into Michigamua, the University's secret society, and begin to learn what C. Wright Mills meant by the power elite.

> In 1960, I hitchhiked to Berkeley, where I bonded with the *Daily Californian*'s editor and students who were battling for their rights to free speech over "off campus" issues, which evolved into the Free Speech Movement. University vice president James Lewis told me that my articles on the new student movement had crossed a line, that such rhetoric could lead to the excesses of Hitler and Mussolini. Ignoring the warning, I published editorials endorsing the creation of a student political party; that led to VOICE, the first chapter of Students for a Democratic Society.

> In fall 1960, five of us signed a letter to candidates John Kennedy and Richard Nixon calling for "a national youth corps serving in constructive peacetime activity abroad in place of military service." One of us, undergraduate David Mcleod, handed the letter to Kennedy as he prepared to give his speech on the Michigan Union steps on October 14. Kennedy said he would speak to the issue that evening. The Peace Corps was born that night.

> In early 1961, several women students brought us affidavits alleging that the dean of women was snooping into their personal lives, including interracial dating. We turned the documents over to a faculty committee, which, after four months, issued a scathing report calling for reform. We shuddered as our story broke in the *Daily* on May 30, 1961, as my time as editor came to an end. The dean of women resigned shortly after.

> The 1961 U.S. debacle at Cuba's Bay of Pigs and the Cuban capture of an American U-2 pilot spying on the island led to a huge controversy over Kennedy administration "news management," which is of even greater significance in today's "war on terror" debates. The president

asserted a government "duty of self-interest" to manipulate the news during a military crisis; the Pentagon spokesman, Arthur Sylvester, declared the "inherent right of a government to lie to save itself." As outgoing *Daily* editor, I rallied with student editors across the country against the rise of news management, including a natural tendency of young editors to censor themselves.

The point of this is that if you were at the *Daily* you couldn't escape the real world by living in a parenthesis or bubble. The real world came knocking when you were reporting and writing editorials every day.

All that was happening as I left the *Daily* 54 years ago, and has been recurring in ups and downs ever since, as this splendid book of memories points out in detail.

Looking back, I loved the University then and love it now on a deep sentimental level. As I wrote in an awkward farewell editorial on May 30, 1961 (awkward since it was a rule that journalists never expressed personal feelings), "it is tough to think all darkly of a university that has often been so nice." I had enjoyed losing a putting match with the dean of student relations. I remembered days of "warm blue sun" when it was "very grassy," the "frequent kindnesses" of professors, and how sometimes in class "a professor turned a stirring phrase" and I "caught my mind changing or felt the deep-down chest heat that means a truth is forming there." I wrote that "speaking out without equivocation against the felt wrongs is painful because people are hurt" (I was thinking of the demoted dean of women). But it was necessary "to live the kept pledge and, in living it, wagering on its worth, and in knowing the wager can be lost, but never conclusively won." The desire "to reject it all, to lie down in waiting, to pass the days on seashores" was sometimes overwhelming but had to be rejected.

Those were life lessons—or as they say today, "educational outcomes"—that the *Daily*, and the University that nervously housed us, taught me. Similar lessons have been taken to heart by decades of *Daily* men and women ever since. I only wish in retrospect that I could have appreciated the *Daily*'s long heritage before my time, but I was young, brash, and ignorant of what had come before. That amazing history is well conveyed in *Special to the Daily: The First 100 Years of Editorial Freedom at the Michigan Daily* (Caddo Gap Press, 1990) by my old friend and colleague Susan Holtzer, who compiled key historical articles printed in the *Daily*. The paper declared itself as a "revolution in college

journalism" in its first week of print in 1890, and embarked on directly
covering the entire 20th century and beyond. Wars, depressions, football
scandals, and attempts at censorship came and went so continually that,
reading the commemorative volume a few years ago, I understood that I
was one of many in a long awakening from apathy that the *Daily* tradition
at its best represents. Like myself, each generation repeats the fallacy of
the New, innocent of the rich history from which we came. Who would
know, were it not for the *Daily* archives, that Frederick Douglass spoke
on October 19, 1893, to an "enthusiastic" crowd that filled "little more
than two-thirds" of University Hall? Who knows that the early CIA
thought *Daily* editors might be good spies? For example, Harry Lunn, the
Daily's 1953–54 editor, became a CIA agent and subsequently tried to
recruit other editors and student leaders. In 1959, another *Daily* editor,
Peter Eckstein, directed a summer seminar financed by the CIA and later
edited a magazine financed by the CIA and focused on international
student developments.[2] Who knows that a *Daily* reporter was the first
inside the newly integrated Little Rock Central High School in 1957? Or
that two *Daily* reporters were arrested by Batista's police for trying to get
the first interview with Fidel Castro in 1958?

That intrepid *Daily* spirit was best summarized, I think, in a 1943
editorial signed by the retiring editors, protesting a Board that had
"crippled" the *Daily* by rejecting the students' choice for new editors.
This was during the Second World War, when the right to editorial
freedom was on the line:

> Retiring editors usually write a lot of sentimental tripe in their farewell
> editorial. All we will say is this: fight like hell for what you believe and
> for what you know is right. If you do this, people will either sneer or pat
> you on the head and tell you that you are young and "idealistic." They
> will tell you that the University must be "practical" and train students
> for a "practical world," that there is no place for idealism in a practical
> world. They will tell you this because they are old and tired, dried up,
> stagnant both mentally and morally. They have lost all hope of getting a
> better world and they have lost their faith in the common people and in

---

2. The *New York Times* published a lengthy and positive obituary on Lunn's long career
as an art dealer, only mentioning in three sentences that he was recruited by the CIA during
his senior year, and remained until 1967 with "his cover blown" when *Ramparts* magazine
exposed his involvement with the National Student Association, which was funded in part by
the Agency. The Eckstein story is told by Karen Paget, in *Patriotic Betrayal,* Yale, 2015, p. 230.

freedom. . . . One of the greatest disappointments in our college life was to find men of this kind sprinkled through the faculty of as great a university as Michigan. . . .

The important thing to remember is that you cannot compromise with them, you cannot appease them, you cannot make peace with them. You have to fight, you have to fight every minute and all of the way. And you have to fight like hell.

If these were ghosts, our work surely includes their resurrection. My deepest thanks to Stephanie Steinberg for getting so many "ghostwriters" to pen their memoirs, for editing the work of so many fine journalists, for carrying on the *Daily* tradition, and for signing her request to me, "GO BLUE" (in upper case). Bury me at Maynard.

Tom Hayden was the editor of his high school paper at Royal Oak Dondero and followed his former editor Joni Katz to the *Michigan Daily* in September 1957. He arranged his courses according to the *Daily*'s schedule and was seen sleeping on *Daily* desks occasionally. He covered the University beat in his junior year, allowing him to study classic theories of higher education while seeing the Regents, the governor, and state politicians at close range, often disturbingly for a young idealist. He then served as editor-in-chief and wrote many editorials on the idea of a university. He editorialized for the Peace Corps and against J. Edgar Hoover, which caused the opening of his first FBI file. He wrote his graduate thesis on C. Wright Mills, but left Ann Arbor for the civil rights movement in Georgia, community organizing in Newark, a decade in resistance against the Vietnam War, and two decades in the Jerry Brown administration and the California legislature. He never stopped writing, however, publishing nineteen books over the decades, mostly on historic events he witnessed. Today he is on the editorial board of the *Nation* magazine. His files covering fifty years, including his writings for the *Daily*, are being stored at the University under an agreement that will bring him to campus one week per year in the next five years.

INTRODUCTION

STEPHANIE STEINBERG

On a relatively quiet street in the heart of Ann Arbor sits a two-story brick and stone building with stained-glass windows and a turret that emits a shining light at night.

By day, students pass by on their way to the ivy-covered Michigan Union at one end of Maynard Street, while administrators round the Cube and shuffle by to grab coffee or a quick lunch from the eateries at the other end. By nightfall, the foot traffic ceases. Professors wrap up office hours, students clear out of dining halls, and the lights flicker off in lecture halls.

While the entire University of Michigan campus winds down, the 150 or so college kids inside the warm glow at 420 Maynard, home to the University's largest student-run paper, the *Michigan Daily*, are just starting their night.

There's not one answer why an 18- or 21-year-old is drawn to this building at 2:00 a.m. on a Thursday or 2:00 p.m. on a Sunday. For some, it's the sheer joy they get out of writing and telling stories. For others, it's something to put on their résumé. And yet for most, it's the feeling of belonging and working among a diverse group of peers who share the same daunting goal: to take eight blank pages and fill them with words and photos that tell over 40,000 readers what they should know when they pick up the ink-smeared newsprint each morning.

Since September 29, 1890, thousands of student journalists have dedicated their college nights—and early mornings and afternoons—to produce the articles and images that span the *Daily*.

Many tiptoe up the shadowed staircase and timidly tread through the wood newsroom doors as freshmen, afraid to ask the senior editors where the bathroom is, let alone how to write a nutgraf. The same students often leave with their names at the top of the masthead and a sense of what they want to do with their lives—either pursue journalism or run far, far away from it.

The stories in this book are the tales of those who chose the former. In celebration of the *Daily*'s 125th anniversary, several of the paper's most notable alumni and a few rising journalism stars have revisited the stories and photos that were their front-row seats for witnessing history and made them fall in love with journalism and storytelling. Yet in more cases than not, their passion for the craft sprung only after enduring a bit of strife.

Sara Fitzgerald climbed the journalism ladder from the *St. Petersburg Times* to *National Journal* and the *Washington Post*. But her news judgment was first tested as editor-in-chief of the *Daily* on January 22, 1973, when she faced a feuding staff divided on whether to run Lyndon B. Johnson's death or the Supreme Court's *Roe v. Wade* decision as the lead story the next day. Sara Krulwich has captured thousands of Broadway productions as the *New York Times'* first culture photographer. But before reaching the stage, she defied Michigan officials who barked at her to take her lens and get off the Big House field—as her press pass stated, "No women or children allowed." Today, Geoffrey Gagnon helps decide which stories should run in *GQ* magazine. But as editor-in-chief in 2001, he had to make sense of two planes hitting two towers and decide what should run in the *Daily* on September 12.

Whether they spent four months or four years toiling at the *Michigan Daily*, each alum had a different experience. Some broke international news, like the global scoop when Jonas Salk announced in Rackham Auditorium he had created a safe and effective polio vaccine. Others unknowingly documented historic events, like John F. Kennedy's 2:00 a.m. speech on the Union steps, where he laid out plans for what eventually became the Peace Corps. Dozens of sportswriters traveled some two thousand miles to Pasadena to cover the Wolverines' twenty Rose Bowl games. Pop culture buffs reviewed new Beatles records, the first *Harry Potter* movie and the last *Friends* episode. And the opinion columnists voiced their frustration with the state's marijuana policies and Regents' decision to raise tuition again.

Though the University of Michigan offered a journalism program until 1995, the majority of these writers didn't study journalism and received no formal training in the field. Instead, they learned from an editor only a year or two older how to structure a news story in pyramid style, write an attention-grabbing lede, properly attribute a quote, or adjust a camera's aperture to get the best shot in the Diag. There were no advisers to turn to if an irate professor claimed he was misquoted or if the University's Office of Public Affairs complained a story was misleading. "We had to figure it out ourselves every day," says *Sports Illustrated* writer Michael Rosenberg, the *Daily*'s editor-in-chief in 1995. "Sometimes the process was sloppy, and sometimes the product was sloppy. But the product was ours and, most days, we could be proud of it."

Some outsiders say a million-dollar operation run solely by 18- to 22-year-olds should have an adult in charge so students have someone to turn to when things go awry. But that's the beauty of the *Daily*. There is no one to turn to but each other. The editors, writers, photographers, and designers share the utter frustration, stress, and tears that come with running the paper, but also the triumphant successes as they hurdle over each roadblock together.

There's really no better preparation for covering journalism in the real world. And there's no better "training" than being handed a notebook and recorder and then pushed out the door to cover a game or random campus event.

As Bloomberg's Shannon Pettypiece, who covered the University's complex affirmative action case as a *Daily* reporter in 2002, puts it, "Starting to write for the *Daily* is like being thrown into the deep end of a pool . . . You learned from your mistakes and from the editors, who themselves had been thrown in just a few years before you."

Since the first edition was published under the flag *U of M Daily*, the newspaper has printed the bylines of eight Pulitzer Prize winners and journalists whose stories and photos have graced the front pages of the *New York Times*, *Wall Street Journal*, *Washington Post*, *USA Today*, *Chicago Tribune*, *Detroit Free Press*, and countless other publications across the country and world. Some made the leap from print to TV, or photos to film, like Academy Award–winning film editor Jay Cassidy, who says his days capturing the turbulent 1960's inspired him to tell stories through movies.

It's normal to see these alumni on the trail of presidential campaigns, broadcasting from the sidelines at the Super Bowl, or making the rounds of Sunday morning news shows. Yet most of them would not have reached this point had they not first tested the journalism waters during their college days.

Each alum has a horrifying, comical, or heart-warming tale behind his or her stories that hit campus newsstands, but there's one common thread that runs through the generations of journalists in this book: the *Michigan Daily* is a large reason they chose this tumultuous, yet satisfying, career. As Jeremy Peters, a *New York Times* political reporter who covered the 2000 presidential election for the *Daily*, writes, "It's hard to imagine I would be where I am today without those experiences."

And those one-of-a-kind experiences are partly what keep the residents of 420 Maynard producing a paper night after night, adapting with the evolving printing process. In the 1960's, the rotary press housed in the basement would shake the building when it hit high speed—"usually at four in the morning, so few knew," Cassidy says. "If you didn't have a scar from a flick of hot lead at some point in your *Daily* experience," he adds, "you weren't really putting out the paper." Today, the printing press has disappeared (the paper is printed an hour away in Davisburg, Michigan), and the only harm to students is the eye fatigue caused by staring too long at computer screens. But what goes into filling the pages hasn't changed much.

Walk up to the second story any hour of the day and you'll likely find frantic reporters calling sources on deadline, music blaring, and some worn-out editor napping on a couch in the back. It's one big, chaotic mess of late nights spent tearing apart stories, writing bad headlines, and drinking the *Daily* pop machine's 50-cent Cokes (which were once upon a time only 5 cents). And somehow, out of the mayhem emerges some of the country's finest college journalism and professional journalists.

Yet no matter the decade their byline appeared in, any alum will tell you that as soon the rhythm of producing a daily paper starts, it all too quickly comes to an end.

Each of us eventually leaves 420 Maynard. But as you'll find out through these stories, 420 Maynard never completely leaves us.

Stephanie Steinberg was a *Michigan Daily* copy editor, news reporter, and senior news editor from 2008 to 2010. She served as editor-in-chief in 2011, when she led the production of the *Michigan Daily*'s first book *Michigan Football: A History of the Nation's Winningest Program*. Her bylines have appeared in the *New York Times*, the *Boston Globe*, *USA Today*, CNN.com, the *Oakland Press*, and the *Detroit Jewish News*. After graduation, she worked as the first online Living editor for WTOP radio in Washington, D.C. She is currently an assistant editor of the health and money sections at *U.S. News & World Report*, where the college rankings founder ranked her No. 1 for Most School Spirit.

THE ROAD TO SELMA

ROGER RAPOPORT

March 1965

> "We are on the one yard line. Our backs are to the wall. Do we let them go over for a touchdown or do we raise the Confederate flag as did our forefathers and tell them, 'You shall not pass?'"
>
> —BIRMINGHAM COMMISSIONER OF PUBLIC SAFETY AND SELMA, ALABAMA NATIVE EUGENE "BULL" CONNOR

"Keep Out Or Get Shot"

Looking at the crudely written warning painted on the side of an abandoned bus outside Gadsden, Alabama, I felt a small sense of relief. All the way south from Ann Arbor we'd passed signage damaged by countless spelling errors. It was starting to look like the region was badly in need of vowels. Finally we had found a hate group with a qualified proofreader. Glory Hallelujah.

Demonstrators and reporters from Michigan were the last thing the state of Alabama wanted in March 1965. Locals were getting downright weary of civil rights tourists stirring up the black community.

Brand names like the Reverend Martin Luther King Jr. and his entourage were mouthing off to the "white liberal media" extending an open invitation to hippie demonstrators and Marxists who thought they had the God given right to take on the doctrine of states rights. Whites were happy. Blacks were happy. All you had to do was stop by Governor George Wallace's office in Montgomery to confirm it for yourself.

All that changed when the tragic murders of two civil rights demonstrators suddenly turned Alabama into a national battleground.

Among the many news organizations covering the story that warm winter and spring was the *Michigan Daily* which liked to tell its readers "sometimes we forget we are just a student paper."

At the time it was typical to find a staff reported interview with Selective Service Director Lewis Hershey or Arkansas Senator J. William Fulbright voicing his opposition to the war in Vietnam. Of course the *Daily* never told its readers how we got those big stories.

Because our reporters were unpaid at the time and there was also no expense money, landing one of these plumb assignments was as difficult as putting steam on a mirror. Hitchhiking, sleeping in church basements, and dining with big city reporters kind enough to pick up the tab was all part of the drill.

My journey to the racial battlefield in Selma began unexpectedly in the basement recreation room of South Quad. The catalyst was network coverage of a disastrous civil rights march in this cradle of the confederacy.

While more than half of Dallas County Alabama's 30,000 citizens of voting age were black, just about 300 were registered to vote. This put them at a distinct disadvantage in a county where two-thirds of the white citizenry was registered.

Local registrars used a variety of creative tactics to suppress the black vote. Blacks could only apply to register two days a month with a limit of 15 people approved per day. These applicants had to pass literacy tests and answer questions such as, "How many legislators did South Carolina send to the first U.S. Congress?"

In January 1965 Martin Luther King led the first of a series of protests in Selma prompting many arrests including his own. Among the black prisoners joining him was a 14-year-old-boy who emerged from a two-week sentence to discover his father had been summarily fired.

At the February Selma funeral for murdered civil rights worker Jimmie Lee Jackson plans were announced for a protest march to the state Capitol in Montgomery. Jackson, a 26-year-old church deacon, father, and former soldier, had been shot by a state trooper while attempting to protect his mother and 82-year-old grandfather being assaulted by state troopers in a Marion, Alabama cafe.

While Jackson lay dying at a local Selma hospital from a painful bullet wound in his stomach, State Police Colonel Al Lingo had the young man arrested on assault charges. This event, less than a year after the murder of three civil rights workers struggling to register black voters in neighboring

Mississippi, helped inspire the largest protest march in Alabama history. The idea came from a local minister who proposed delivering Jackson's casket to the state Capitol.

On March 7, more than 600 members of the local black community, along with visiting students, civil rights workers, rabbis, ministers, nuns, lawyers, and doctors, set off on a 54 mile march to Montgomery. Soon these protesters were part of biggest local showdown since confederate forces fell a century earlier in the Battles of Ebenezer Church and the Battle of Selma. The difference this time was that the northerners were unarmed.

Heeding the battle cry of Alabama native son Bull Connor (who earned his place in American history by unleashing police dogs and water cannons on black demonstrators in Birmingham), authorities launched a goal line stand that swept the law-abiding marchers back across the Edmund Pettus Bridge. Within minutes the state troopers, their deputies, and club wielding mounted police cheered on by white spectators, had brutally beaten about 70 demonstrators, including 17 who were hospitalized.

Coverage of Selma's "Bloody Sunday" turned the city into something Bull Connor could have never imagined. ABC interrupted the movie *Judgment At Nuremberg* to broadcast footage of the beatings. Selma became Mecca for a multiracial protest community and a parking lot for network television trucks. Federal Judge Frank Johnson Jr. quickly issued a temporary restraining order against further police action and new marches while he reviewed one of the most brutal attacks in American civil rights history.

Among the many clergy who responded to Reverend King's call following the Sunday attacks was a 38-year-old social worker and Unitarian minister, James Reeb. The American Friends Service Committee worker had recently moved to a low income neighborhood in Boston, where he enrolled his children in a biracial public school.

On March 9, Reeb and other ministers joined hundreds of local blacks for a new Selma protest. Following an evening prayer service, he headed to dinner with two fellow ministers. On their way back to their lodgings the men were attacked by a white mob. Convinced that he would be turned away at the city's whites-only hospital, local civil rights leaders rushed Reeb to an infirmary for black patients. He died of head injuries two days later at a Birmingham hospital.

The murder of this white minister had far more national impact than the killing of black demonstrator Jimmie Lee Jackson weeks earlier.

President Lyndon B. Johnson called Reeb's widow to offer his sympathy and arranged for a plane to fly the victim's father in from Wyoming.

On March 15, President Johnson proposed a new Voting Rights Act:

> "There is no issue of States rights or national rights," he told a joint session of Congress. "There is only the struggle for human rights . . . We have already waited a hundred years and more, and the time for waiting is gone . . . Their cause must be our cause too. Because it is not just Negroes, but really it is all of us, who must overcome the crippling legacy of bigotry and injustice. And we shall overcome."

Hours after Johnson's speech, a federal district judge issued a permit approving a Selma demonstration the following day. Among the news organization on scene for that historic event was the *Michigan Daily*.

My overnight drive to Alabama on March 15 was made courtesy of University of Michigan students eager to join the protest. Traveling light, with only a change of clothes and a toothbrush, this journey in the back of a cramped Ford was a quick introduction to national reporting. Everywhere we went people were asking similar questions.

At a McDonald's in Lexington, Kentucky, a clerk couldn't understand why I was trying to get directions south to Birmingham. Didn't we realize there were no spring break beaches in Birmingham.

"What the hell you wanna go down there for?"

In Harriman, Tennessee, a gas station attendant took one look at our Michigan plates and gave us his thumbnail view of the Yankee news media.

"I think it's mostly those damn outsiders causing all the trouble—it's like Governor Wallace says: 'You can't trust the newspapers. They always leave out the stuff about a bunch of n—— raping a white woman.'"

Our group left without bothering to wait for free green stamps.

At our first gas stop in Alabama, a queue gathered to stare at our Michigan plates. Down the road billboards asked: "What's wrong with being right? Join the Birch Society and fight Communism and Socialism."

Rolling past "It's Nice to Have You In Birmingham" signs I noticed a number of passing motorists staring at us. There were quick side glances, long glaring looks, short smirks, and many frowns.

At another stop we looked away when a gas station attendant asked, "Where you going, Fort Lauderdale?"

My biggest concern was being pulled over by police and missing out on the big story. Only when we reached Selma—"a great place to visit, a better place to live"—was it clear why we hadn't seen an Alabama state trooper for six hours.

Most of the force had been assigned to a blockade set up on Sylvan Street in the heart of Selma's black community. Beige state police cars displaying confederate flags were everywhere. One front bumper had a picture of a grizzled confederate veteran. "Hell no, I ain't fergettin'."

These officers were supplemented by gray and brown vehicles from the city and state police. Heading the battalion was a red '52 Chevy sound truck occupied by a sleeping driver.

When I inquired about a press pass a stranger suggested it might make more sense to board a train leaving Selma. Inside the restroom green Dallas courthouse I was handed my pass in a plastic holder along with a fictitious smear article contending that Martin Luther King was a communist and his top aide, Rev. Ralph Abernathy, had recently seduced a 15-year-old girl.

On the desk of Sheriff Jim Clark was a photo showing him wrestling with a plus size black woman. Two bulletin boards were filled with telegrams about his successful Bloody Sunday effort to whip, club, and gas law-abiding demonstrators into submission. They ran the gamut from "Way to go Jim, Give 'em Hell" to "I protest your Gestapo tactics, you are worse than Hitler."

Claiming he had been threatened by local blacks, the sheriff was temporarily living at the county jail for his own safety. Among his critics was Wilson Baker, the city's public safety director who told me that he had almost quit after the Bloody Sunday beatings.

"I don't want anyone to get hurt," he said. "We're going to play this thing by ear. I will always obey any court order."

That hot afternoon I reported on Reverend Martin Luther King's eulogy for Reverend Reeb at the packed Brown Chapel A.M.E. Church:

"His crime was that he dared live his faith . . . He was murdered by the timidity of a federal government that can spend millions of dollars a day to keep troops in South Vietnam, yet cannot protect the lives of its own citizens seeking constitutional civil rights."

Shortly before the service ended, U.S. District Judge Daniel H. Thomas approved an eight block march through the center of town. Over 3,000 demonstrators from Selma and across the country were given state and local police protection. This voter rights demonstration was applauded by United Auto Workers president Walter Reuther who had also come down from Michigan to call for the entire country to mobilize behind these demonstrators.

"We must mobilize people from Michigan to Mississippi to give the right to vote to all people," he said.

On March 21, a federal court sanctioned a new march from Selma to Montgomery under National Guard protection. Camping in the back yards of their local supporters, serenaded by singers such as Harry Belafonte and Lena Horne, the demonstrators were joined en route by three assistant U.S. Attorney Generals. Governor Wallace and local police were enjoined from harassing the marchers.

By the time a crowd of 25,000 voting rights demonstrators reached Montgomery on March 25, Rev. King sensed victory: "We must come to see that the end we seek is a society at peace with itself, a society that can live with its conscience."

That night, while driving a Selma demonstrator back home from the capitol, Michigan volunteer and activist Viola Liuzzo was murdered by four Ku Klux Klansmen.

Five months later Congress responded to the tragic events in Selma by passing the Voting Rights Act.

Four suspects were arrested in the murder of Rev. James Reeb. One did not have to stand trial, while the others were acquitted by a jury of white men.

In the Liuzzo murder case, all four suspects were acquitted by a state jury. Two were subsequently convicted on federal charges while a third entered a witness protection program on a plea bargain.

James Fowler, the state trooper who shot unarmed Jimmie Lee Jackson in the stomach, pleaded guilty to second-degree manslaughter and served a six month sentence in 2010 and 2011.

Two summers after Selma I returned to Montgomery, Alabama to join the staff of the *Southern Courier*, a student-run civil rights newspaper. Week after week our staff reported more stories about the continuing civil rights battles across the South. During that tour of duty I visited and interviewed Governor Wallace who gave me his autographed picture. In June I returned to Michigan in plenty of time to spend a week covering the Detroit race riots for the *Wall Street Journal*.

Half a century later, little Selma remains a big tour stop on the southern civil rights trail. Today, of course, there are still reporters in other countries finding safety in church basements and perhaps hitchhiking part of the way home from human rights stories the way I did. The *Daily*'s coverage of those events was part of a long tradition that confirmed our paper's commitment to eyewitness reporting.

The suppression of voter rights, not just those of blacks but all Americans, remains on the national agenda. Part of this discussion was triggered by the Supreme Court's decision to gut portions of the Voting Rights Act in 2013. The disenfranchisement of some voters, inside and outside the South, remains a widely covered story. The *Michigan Daily* remains a good place to continue following this national story that impacts all of us.

Roger Rapoport was a *Michigan Daily* news reporter from 1964 to 1967 and editor from 1967 to 1968. He has written for the *San Francisco Chronicle*, *Los Angeles Times*, *Chicago Tribune*, *Harper's*, and the *Atlantic*. His books include *Citizen Moore*, *Hillsdale*, and *Pilot Error*, which is the basis of his feature film released in 2015. The lead character in *Pilot Error* is investigative reporter Nicola Wilson, who began her career at the *Michigan Daily*. He is also the producer of the feature film *Waterwalk*. Rapoport lives in Muskegon, Michigan, with his wife Marty Ferriby, director of the Hackley Public Library since 1994.

F8 AND BE THERE

ANDY SACKS

October 15, 1965

I thought I would be a good sport about it. Take the photo assignment that was handed to me, the freshman photographer, and do what I could with it. The big event of that day, October 15, 1965, was supposed to be the University of Michigan homecoming parade and a concert that evening. Those assignments went to more experienced *Daily* photographers. They knew the ropes, and, as I understood it, the parade and the homecoming hoopla were not going to be their first rodeos.

On the other hand, I had been at college for only six weeks. Born in December, I was almost eighteen years old by mid-October 1965. So as the new kid on the staff, I headed down Liberty Street toward Main, on foot, to see what a sit-in at the Selective Service office was all about.

In today's parlance, I was the low value asset deployed for this low priority event. The paper needed to have some photo coverage of the demonstration, but why send the top guys to staff it? After all, what is the action at a sit-in? The people all sit down. So I thought.

I owned one secondhand Asahi Pentax camera, bought toward the end of my service on the Berkley High School *Spectator* staff, and two extra preset Spiratone lenses. Together, the lenses, a 135mm telephoto and a 28mm wide angle, cost less than $80. I carried all of it in an army green canvas shoulder bag that I thought helped me look rough and ready. I was 6 feet tall and weighed almost 150 pounds with camera gear. Maybe ready, but not rough. (The irony of carrying a faux army issue shoulder bag to a draft board sit-in did not occur to me until I sat down to write this piece.)

So I got to the sit-in and found everyone sitting down. It was just like it sounds—you go in somewhere, and you sit. The only shot I saw for the first couple of hours was to juxtapose the profile of an elderly secretary sitting straight and rigid at her desk intently typing, with the protesters sitting against file cabinets behind her.

My sympathies slightly favored the protesters who were mostly students. I myself had chosen to study art and design, in part to diminish my chances of being drafted. There were "student deferments" in that era, which excused young men from the military draft if they were in college.

Equally important to me was the opportunity to major in photography. That study would commence in my sophomore year, once I had the basic art and drawing requirements satisfied.

But on this Friday afternoon in 1965, I had "excused myself" from my formal studies to cover the protesters at the draft board office sit-in.

The afternoon moved slowly. At one point, Ann Arbor Police Chief Walter Krasny, in a jacket and tie, was in the office, peacefully smiling, as a helmeted officer stood nearby. Two other photographers were also stationed in the office. As the four o'clock hour came and went, the tension inside the office increased.

Officially, the Selective Service office staff had no beef with the protesters' political opinions. However, privately, the staff was loyal to their employer, the United States military.

The deep divide between town and gown in 1965 Ann Arbor was not a secret. But I had been living in West Quad for six weeks, so it was news to me. And as an art student, unschooled in the fundamentals of the peace movement, a lot of the nuance was over my head. (Twenty years later in my career, I would joke with other photogs about everything a successful news photographer needed to know: *f8 and be there.*)

Normally, the Selective Service office staff worked like a machine, methodically notifying kids for wartime service. When five o'clock rolled around, they locked up the office and headed home. But there were thousands of records of all the eligible draft-age men in Washtenaw County in files, and today the staff was not going to leave three dozen peaceniks, strangers hell-bent to make a political statement, alone in the office all weekend.

So the authorities were called in to tell the protesters they would be arrested for trespassing if they didn't get up and move out. Nobody budged.

The city police came first. The county sheriff deputies backed a paddy wagon van up to the Liberty Street doorway. The office was upstairs, so

Photo by Andy Sacks.

every one of the demonstrators had to be carried out of the office and down the stairs by two or three cops.

A newbie, I was both empowered and informed by watching how a TV news crew and other photographers were handling themselves at this point. This was my first rodeo. Even so, I quickly realized there were two main areas of activity accessible to photograph. Without knowing or ever having used the term, I had started a shot list.

Shot No. 1: Upstairs in the office, as police grabbed sitting protesters in a semi-careful manner to pick them up off the floor.

Shot No. 2: When police carried the limp, non-violent bodies out the front door to the waiting paddy wagon.

The trip down the stairs was not an easy or a safe shot to attempt. Poor sight angles and the ever-challenging maneuver of walking backwards down a flight of stairs, while focusing and shooting an unpredictable situation, was too much to handle. And so far, the police had not gotten rowdy with me, so I was mindful of staying out of their way to get my job done.

Uptown, violinist Yehudi Menuhin was playing a concert at Hill Auditorium.

Downtown, I had figured out a way to climb up three feet on a street light pole to get an elevated view over the sea of helmets on the street. The footing wasn't ideal, but it worked.

Across Liberty Street a second story window opened above Hutzel's clothing store.

Shot No. 3: I made my way into that building and rested the Pentax with the 28mm Spiratone wide angle lens on the open windowsill to steady it. I ran a bracket of long time exposures centered at f8 at 1 second showing the deputies ringing the building entrance, lit only by street lamps.

Eventually, all 39 protesters were carried out, arrested, and taken off to jail that night.

Two of my photos ran on page one in the Saturday morning paper.

After that, I was ready for my next rodeo.

I never again learned so much by skipping class.

Andy Sacks was a *Michigan Daily* photographer from 1965 to 1969. He graduated in May 1969 with a bachelor of science in design from the College of Architecture and Design. He has been a freelance photojournalist since 1970. His print and video work has appeared in media throughout the world. He recently completed a documentary called *Let's Have Some Church Detroit Style* that will be released in 2015. He lives in Chelsea, Michigan, with his wife Ann.

PRIMARY SOURCES:
CAPTURING KENNEDY IN DETROIT

JAY CASSIDY

May 16, 1968

The *Michigan Daily* had always been the nexus of a certain energy and activity on campus, but, as the turbulent times of the 1960's in this country played out at the University of Michigan and the streets of Ann Arbor, the paper's relevance grew with a more challenged and committed readership.

The two big issues of the day—civil rights and the Vietnam War—were accompanied by the trauma of the assassination of President John F. Kennedy, riots in the inner cities (politely referred to as "civil unrest"), the weekly tally of Americans and Vietnamese killed in the conflict overseas, and the murders of Martin Luther King Jr. and Robert Kennedy less than three months apart. It was a time of political and social fracture and re-examination which can best be summed up in the Chinese curse: "May you live in interesting times."

They were. And we, at the *Daily*, were interested, challenging, and irreverent. If there was an operating principle at the *Michigan Daily* at that time it was another Chinese curse: "May you come to the attention of those in authority."

Nearly 40 years later, the negatives from my time as a *Daily* photographer from 1967 to 1970 lay in non-acid-free envelopes in wooden cases in a Public Storage facility in West Los Angeles. In November 2006, I received an email from Nancy Bartlett, an archivist at the Bentley Historical Library in Ann Arbor, outlining the idea for The Michigan Daily Photographers Project, which proposed to collect photos from former *Daily* photographers.

Nancy wrote: "By contributing a selection of up to 50 of your favorite images, you will be adding significantly to the visual memory of the campus."

Good idea. I started scanning the black and white 35mm negatives to digital files, looking for those 50 favorites. A conundrum occurred right away. Since I had few contact sheets, I had to put each frame through the scanner just to figure out what the image was.

These photographs were taken, processed, selected, and prepared for publication on a daily deadline. And I was not always the person making the selection—the lab work rotated among the photographers and the current photo editor.

A daily newspaper is interested in photographs for news value, looking for one or two representational images that complement the story and express the essence of the event. By definition, the context defines the choice, and the person selecting will pass over many fine images that are either redundant or beyond the mandate. Once photos were selected and the deadline passed, the negatives were set aside without much further consideration.

My first scans became an investigation and a bit of a revelation. Forty years after they were taken, I found myself proposing to "edit" them. But, by being forced to scan the whole roll in order to see what was there, it became very clear that these photographs have much more value unedited than edited.

I could judge the aesthetic value, a good composition, an interesting face, a significant action. But by making a selection, I was putting the photographs into a context—a context defined by me and my memories.

My choice would be an interpretation that included some images and excluded others. But why limit what some future viewer or researcher might find interesting or revealing?

So I made the decision to scan every frame—the favorites, the not-so-favorites, the technically deficient and the mis-fires—down to the roll-outs.

A decision that had a large personal downside: I had to scan every frame and anyone who's used a Nikon negative scanner will have sympathy. With long interruptions for the business of life, it took me until 2010 to finish this project.

The 50 "favorite" photographs that Nancy hoped to receive became over 4,000.

When looking at some of these photographs in the order they went through the camera, stories emerge. Stories that we missed in the day because the rush to publish made us focus on selecting one or two images.

Here's what I'm talking about:

In the spring of 1968, Senator Robert F. Kennedy made a bid to be the Democratic nominee for president. He entered the race after Senator Eugene McCarthy found strong support from those who opposed the Vietnam War and from those who had less to gain by the continuation of the status quo. By definition, these groups were young people.

In January 1968, the Tet Offensive revealed a different narrative that further unmasked the official government line about the Vietnam War—good news being defined as body counts and villages deemed sympathetic. President Lyndon B. Johnson announced his decision not to seek re-election at the end of March. The vice president, Hubert H. Humphrey, was less the heir-apparent than the guy who had been forced to hold his tongue for the past four years as Vietnam slid further and further off the rails. The nomination field was open.

The Kennedy campaign encouraged student journalists around the country. We made one trip to cover the campaign in Indianapolis at the beginning of May. For the May 16, 1968 visit to Detroit, the *Daily* obtained credentials for two photographers—Andrew Sacks and myself. Why the campaign agreed to two credentials for the same publication probably had to do with some sleight of hand on our part. (Sacks may have represented another news entity.) But it was clear why we both wanted to participate. This was national news. The momentum gained by the Kennedy campaign had much to do with the evolution of the candidate. He had grown from being perceived as his brother's "enforcer" as attorney general, to Lyndon Johnson's nemesis, to carpetbagger senator from New York, to a presidential candidate who questioned the government line on the war, and asked to be the voice of the disadvantaged and disenfranchised.

No one who heard his emotional speech on the evening of April 4, 1968, a few hours after Martin Luther King Jr. was shot and killed in Memphis, could doubt that this candidate would move the country in a different direction.

Kennedy said: "And let's dedicate ourselves to what the Greeks wrote so many years ago: to tame the savageness of man and make gentle the life of this world. Let us dedicate ourselves to that, and say a prayer for our country and for our people."

Here are a few frames from that *Daily* assignment in Detroit on May 16. These frames were not chosen to illustrate the story in the next day's *Daily* and have never been published. And you see something in them I couldn't comprehend then—the unmistakable evidence of the depth of extremist hate directed at Kennedy three weeks before his assassination.

The right-wing group that carried the hate signs and the black umbrella in the glass case was called "Breakthrough," and it was founded by a Detroit Parks and Recreation Department employee named Donald Lobsinger. On March 14, the group demonstrated against Martin Luther King Jr. who was at Grosse Pointe High School giving a speech.

At the Kennedy rally, where an estimated 10,000 people gathered, the group handed out flyers to the crowd that said: "ROBERT F. KENNEDY TO RECEIVE 'UMBRELLA OF BRITISH PRIME MINISTER NEVILLE CHAMBERLAIN.'"

Robert Kennedy's father, Joseph, had been ambassador to the United Kingdom in the late 1930's and emerged as a supporter of Chamberlain—who often toted a black umbrella—and his policy toward Germany. Domestically, Joe Kennedy became known as an "appeaser" as the events drew the United States closer and closer to war. The black umbrella tarred the father, and clever protesters were not above using it to tar the son.

Five years prior, another clever protester had been in Dealey Plaza yards away from President John F. Kennedy's motorcade at the moment of his assassination. The black umbrella on the clear, sunny day became a favorite of the conspiracy theories that surrounded the assassination. It wasn't until a House Select Committee on Assassinations hearing in 1978 that the "umbrella man" came forward and testified to his use of the black umbrella to remind the son that the legacy of his father was not forgotten.

The Breakthrough group handed out another flyer that day in Detroit. The language of this one could perhaps be dismissed as political hyperbole: "Let Mr. Robert F. Kennedy render a real service, not only to his country but to all mankind, by donating HIS blood—ALL OF IT—to the Viet Cong. And the SOONER, the BETTER." Three weeks later, the intention of the words became reality.

What to make of all this? Not for me to say. Only to consider that the value of the photograph as a primary source is not to be denied.

But something else happened that day.

Photo by Jay Cassidy.

It can be seen in the faces of the people who greeted the candidate. Ten months earlier, Detroit had experienced urban unrest—the "blind pig" riot—that was as brutal as any civil disturbance this country had ever seen. The scale of the riots was only surpassed by the New York City Draft Riots during the Civil War.

Such events took a toll on Detroit, which had seen a dramatic demographic shift, accelerating during World War II through the 40's and 50's. It was a common story in post-war America. The second generation immigrant population moved from the inner city to the suburbs; a different population, fleeing limited opportunities, found its way to northern cities and the manufacturing base.

What happened that day was hope. Or maybe a release from the trauma of the riots. Kennedy's message resonated among those in the crowd, and the outpouring of enthusiasm was evident when I examined the unedited rolls of photographs. Taken together, these photographs reveal a feeling. Feelings may not be of much use to a historian, but evidence appears in many forms.

Looking back, I think my choice of profession was informed by this

Photo by Jay Cassidy.

Photo by Jay Cassidy.

Photo by Jay Cassidy.

Photo by Jay Cassidy.

Photo by Jay Cassidy.

desire to create contexts for the telling of stories with pictures. And I sensed then that working for a newspaper or magazine would not be the right venue for that aspiration.

So, movies it became.

Jay Cassidy was a *Michigan Daily* photographer from 1967 to 1970. He is a motion picture film editor who began his career in the 1970's working on documentaries and political advertisements. He has edited more than thirty films. His most recent credits, *American Hustle* (2013) and *Silver Linings Playbook* (2012), were nominated for ten and eight Academy Awards respectively, including Best Achievement in Film Editing for both films. Cassidy has collaborated with Sean Penn on all the films Penn has directed, most notably *Into the Wild* (2007), for which he was nominated for an Academy Award for Best Achievement in Film Editing. Other credits include *Fury* (2014), *Foxcatcher* (2014) and *An Inconvenient Truth* (2006), which won the Academy Award for Best Documentary. Cassidy won the *New Yorker* Cartoon Caption Contest #39, February 27, 2006. The winning entry ran in the March 27, 2006, issue of the *New Yorker*.

LOUSY STUDENT,
LOUSIER STUDENT JOURNALIST

DANIEL OKRENT

August 26–29, 1968

In the spring and summer of 1968, as the nation boiled with unrest, dislocation, and generational conflict, I was the *Daily*'s national political correspondent. I don't think anyone called me that (except maybe my mother), but it's a reasonable description of part of my life in the year I turned 20. Other descriptors that would be equally accurate: lousy bridge player, lousier student, poseur.

Rubber bridge was the post-deadline pastime at 420 Maynard in those days. My nightly participation didn't mean I particularly liked playing bridge. I played because it was the best way to avoid going home to sleep. That, in turn, explains why I was such a lousy student: I rarely made it to class, and on those occasions when I did, you would likely find me in the back row, nodding off.

Another reason I was a lousy student: At those sporadic instances when I was actually functioning, I was on the road, usually with photographer Andy Sacks. Andy and I covered various marches and other events in Washington, Bobby Kennedy's campaign in the Indiana primary, and the giddy Wisconsin balloting that took place on the heels of Lyndon B. Johnson's shocking withdrawal from the presidential race. And all of that was prelude to the year's big event, the Democratic National Convention in Chicago.

That's where I demonstrated my chops as a poseur. (This photograph may indicate that I was even inclined to pose in the nude. But I'm fairly certain I was wearing shorts—even though the expression on Eric

25

The *Daily* Chicago bureau, August 1968. In front, Jay Cassidy; middle row from left, Pat O'Donohue, Andy Sacks, Eric Pergeaux; back, Tom Copi, John Gray, Leslie Wayne, Dan Okrent.

Pergeaux's face suggests a thought along the lines of "There he goes again," and Pat O'Donohue looks as if she's utterly revolted by something that *somebody* is doing.)

My especially ostentatious displays did not take place in the Holiday Inn near Lake Shore Drive, where all eight of us spent the three nights of the convention in this single room (thus the mattresses on the floor). When it was time to work, the *Daily*'s pop-up bureau hit the streets and parks of Chicago. I, official credentials in hand, put on a suit, a (relatively) clean shirt, and a tie, and went to the International Amphitheater for the convention itself. I was Johnny Deadline, Serious Political Reporter.

For most of the convention's four days I sat in the press gallery, tugging my chin, and gravely considering the urgent business taking place on the floor below. Once, I sidled up to NBC News correspondent Sander Vanocur and attempted to indicate my political savvy by trying to engage him in a conversation about some inconsequential maneuver involving the South Dakota (or was it Idaho?) delegation. Vanocur looked at me as if I had farted, and walked away.

Occasionally, when events had gotten deeply boring and the legitimate reporters had lost interest, I was able to secure a pass that allowed me onto the convention floor. I loitered near the Michigan delegation, looking serious while I scribbled notes about god knows what. I crowded near TV reporters as they interviewed prominent Democrats, hoping to get in the frame of the picture the cameraman had composed. At one point, I walked past the Illinois delegation, asked Chicago Mayor Richard Daley a fatuous question, and got a shouted one-sentence reply. Needless to say, the piece I wrote included a line that began, "I asked Mayor Daley the other day. . . ."

In the meantime, as I played at being a big-time reporter, my friends were witnessing the anti-war, anti-Democrat demonstrations in Grant Park and Lincoln Park, the police riot on Michigan Avenue, the shards of plate glass flying into the lobby of the Chicago Hilton. On the same *Daily* front page that carried my thumbsucker on the mayor's political clout (about which I knew very little that wasn't pure cliché), John Gray wrote about a "club-swinging, tear-gas drenched melee." In my suit, my official credentials, and my somewhat comical and very pretentious self-regard, I had missed the real story.

Daniel Okrent arrived in Ann Arbor on August 28, 1965, dropped off his toothbrush and his clothing at his dorm, and then went straight to the *Daily*; for the next four years, he barely left the building, working successively as sports reporter, news reporter, movie reviewer, arts editor, and feature editor. His nearly half-century in the word business has included stints as editor-in-chief of Harcourt Brace Jovanovich, corporate editor-at-large of Time Inc., and the first public editor of the *New York Times*. His books include *Great Fortune: The Epic of Rockefeller Center* (a finalist for the 2004 Pulitzer Prize in history) and the best-selling *Last Call: The Rise and Fall of Prohibition*. He is also coauthor of the off-Broadway hit *Old Jews Telling Jokes*. When the University of Michigan honored him with an honorary doctorate in 2014, a friend said, "Rather than give you a brand-new degree, why don't they just raise your grades on the old one?"

1969: THE YEAR OF LIVING DANGEROUSLY

JOHN PAPANEK

1969

Two centuries' worth of callow, cocksure, clueless freshmen have arrived in an Ann Arbor September only to be roused, awakened, stimulated, shocked, mind-blown, by their early encounters with the swirling circus of delights and distractions that is the University of Michigan. Members of almost any class could surely make a case for why their first-year stories are the most memorable. On behalf of my sisters and brothers from the Class of '73 (or, as many of us preferred the name we called ourselves in high school, the '69ers), I submit that ours might deserve to top the list.

In our crazy case, just the first *three months* played out with more daily drama and emotion than most other classes experienced in a full four years. And it was *Michigan Daily* drama and emotion as well, as all of it was chronicled by—as it was being *lived* by—the students who formed the family of the greatest college newspaper in the land. (It still makes for great reading in Google's newspaper archives.) I was not part of the *Daily* family as a freshman, but getting to know it and become part of it was the very best thing about Michigan for me, and on day one of my sophomore year I went to 420 Maynard to sign up, after which I hardly ever left—until I had to.

Thanks to so much of what our upper classmates had done and gone through during the crucial run-up years of '66 to '68, September 1969 seemed, to us at least, to be the launch date for every kind of freedom imaginable—social, sexual, cultural, musical, academic, pharmaceutical— and nobody could tell us what we could *not* do, least of all the stuffy

University administrators in the brand new brick fortress built to house and protect them from us, or the bureaucrats who thought they ran things from Lansing and, for that matter, Washington, D.C.

From September through November '69, the University raged and seethed in an endless series of battles, running from cold to very, very hot—between students and administrators; students and landlords; students and other students; students and police; administrators and faculty; townies and the University community. Just as Richard Nixon would gaze out his White House window and wonder whether the heaving sea of protesters and pacifists would ever go away, or at least get haircuts, so too did University President Robben Fleming, an otherwise lovely, anti-war liberal former labor relations expert, wonder how and when his worst nightmare would ever end.

Things had started going south for Fleming—as well as Ann Arbor's mayor, its police chief, Washtenaw County Sheriff Doug Harvey (our own local J. Edgar Hoover), and the eight elected members of the University Board of Regents—the previous summer, though most of us freshmen knew about none of it (nor did many upperclassmen other than those who stuck it out in A² through the May to August trimester) until the first *Daily* issue of the fall semester clued us in. The pertinent page one headlines:

A brief review of summer in the city: Bookstore defeated, ROTC bombed, Rent strike eases

City in crisis: the mayor vs. everyone

'U' to comply with requests by probe of campus unrest

What we needed to know—and fast—was that:

1. The hottest political issue on campus was the demand, expressed overwhelmingly in a March '69 referendum, to establish a student-run bookstore that would offer textbooks at "fair prices," that is, below those set for generations by oligarchic proprietors such as Follett's and Ulrich's. In its July meeting, the Regents rejected the idea out of hand.
2. A close-second hot-button was the continued presence of a Reserve Officers' Training Corp unit, using University facilities, money, and prestige in training students for service in the military, and

supporting a war that was now abhorred by a vast majority of the community. On June 1, a bomb at North Hall, ROTC headquarters, took out a wall and an army staff car.

3. Several court actions were proceeding in a prolonged and tangled fight between students who lived in off-campus apartments and predatory landlords.

4. In mid-June, police busted up a block party organized by a communal group called Trans-Love Energies, founded by the poet John Sinclair, who also started the White Panther Party and served as its minister of information. Trans-Love's mission was to "spread the Cultural Revolution though sex in the streets, dope, and rock 'n roll." Doing it all—quite literally—on South University, just up the block from Fleming's official residence, brought down some 300 helmeted cops with tear gas and riot sticks, arresting 45 people. Sheriff Harvey proudly vowed to continue protecting "the decent people of this area" from "the dope heads, sex nuts, and public drunks." Sinclair was soon sent off to prison to begin serving a 9½- to 10-year prison sentence for giving two marijuana joints to undercover cops. (Only 30 months later, in December 1971, the fight to free Sinclair climaxed with a historic rally and mega-concert in a sold-out Crisler Arena. Movement leaders Jerry Rubin, Bobby Seale, Allen Ginsberg, and a stream of performers including Bob Seger and Phil Ochs steadily heated the crowd of 15,000 until Stevie Wonder and surprise guests John Lennon and Yoko Ono took the stage for a finale that ignited a full-on firestorm. Astonishingly, three days later the Michigan Supreme Court released Sinclair—and changed the state's marijuana laws.)

5. A special State Senate investigating committee was requiring all Michigan colleges and universities to submit information about student political groups on their campuses and their plans for handling disruptions. Sample questions: "What black-only groups exist on your campus? What is the name of your black student group (or groups); estimate size? What are the white political action groups on your campus, i.e. YAF, SDS? Which do you feel are radical?"

There was lot for us all to take in. We knew that football was still big at Michigan—it had the biggest stadium in America—but we didn't know much about the new coach. Glenn E. "Bo" Schembechler, a freshman himself and just 40 years old, would be taking over a mediocre program and hoping to avoid the embarrassment of playing before too many empty seats in cavernous Michigan Stadium, not yet known as the Big House. About all we knew of Bo was that he was coming up from someplace called Miami—wait, *of Ohio?!*—to replace Chalmers "Bump" Elliott, beloved even though the Wolverines languished in the Big Ten's bottom five for most of his 10 seasons. We didn't know what to think when we learned that Schembechler's only tenuous claim to fame—or infamy—was his five-year stint as an assistant to the reviled Woody Hayes at Ohio State. *Daily* sportswriters almost never referred to Hayes without adding their favorite appositive for him, "Fat Boy." If nothing else, we thought it would be interesting to see how Bo would do against his rotund mentor in the traditional season-ending border war between the two squads, this year to be played on November 22 in Michigan Stadium. The '68 renewal, in Columbus, had been a 50–14 Buckeye slaughter, after which they thrashed Southern California in the Rose Bowl finishing the season being hailed not only as the No. 1 team in America, but also perhaps the greatest college team of all time. They were expected to be better in '69.

We had two September weeks of classes before football would begin, not that classes were our top priority. From our first moments on campus all the way through Thanksgiving recess, there would be a "mass meeting"—a polite way (I guessed) of saying "protest rally"—practically every day, beginning on the Diag and sometimes moving on to other destinations. (Actually, the protests almost exclusively happened on weekdays. Saturdays and Sundays we hewed to ancient student tradition, and partied.) As a rule, turnout at the rallies would be modest on Mondays, maybe 150 or 200 people, but it would grow as the week wore on. By Thursdays, the numbers would swell to 500 or more, and draw not only students, but also plenty of local "street people" and even faculty members.

Angry rhetoric demanding the Regents' reconsideration of the student bookstore proposal would generally lead the proceedings, with a Student Government Council leader commanding the bullhorn, the peoples' weapon of choice. After 10 or 15 minutes, as the crowd and its temperature swelled, others would demand their turns on the horn, and over the course of an hour or two we might hear bleating for one cause or another from leaders of Students for a Democratic Society, the White Panthers, Black Berets, Radical Caucus, International Socialists, Radical Lesbians, Young Democrats, Tenants Union, Anarchist Society, Black

Student Union, New Mobilization Committee to End the War in Vietnam (New Mobe, in *Daily* speak), and more. Whether or not all those groups got their daily moments in the pulpit, their samizdat covered virtually every bulletin board, wall, kiosk, lamp post, tree, and Volkswagen bumper in the greater campus area.

Political fragmentation was a problem throughout "the movement," and though the constant chaos of confused leadership of the left was catnip to the relatively few campus conservatives like the Young Americans for Freedom and the student spies reporting back to the FBI, the mounting anger from the Diag was rapidly metastasizing into threatening action. As the Diag rallies grew throughout the week with ever more students and speakers, all growing angrier and bolder, by Friday the crowd would inevitably spill out through the Engineering Arch onto South University, screaming and chanting for *power to the people* and an end to the *effing war* and *racism* and *sexism* and *bookstore price-gouging*, banging drums and cymbals and gongs and—just as inevitably—someone or two picking up a rock or a brick and hurling it through a front window of Ulrich's or Follett's, or a particularly favorite target, the South U. branch of Ann Arbor Bank. A long-lasting impression of our time in Ann Arbor was the sight, those early weeks of Fall '69, of the South U. Ann Arbor Bank branch boarded up with plywood throughout each weekend, new glass going in by Wednesday, then the whole brick-shatter-plywood-new glass pageant playing out again beginning with the next Friday march. After four or five repetitions, the bank wised up and replaced its plate glass *permanently* with steel shutters.

Of course the University had already realized the dangers to those who live behind too much glass. It had recently left its old Administration Building to the softies from the College of Literature, Science, and the Arts. Now the University was governed from a new fortress-like tower, with tiny windows set far back into the brickwork, looking like nothing so much as gun ports. For the record, to this day the University insists that the building, now named for Fleming, who died in 2010, was absolutely *not* designed with repelling student incursions in mind.

For the daily Diag protesters in the Fall of '69, the new Administration Building was indeed a target, and D-Day was approaching. That would be Friday, September 19, when the Regents would meet for the first time in the new trimester, presumably to rule once and for all on the bookstore matter. SGC called for the "cancellation" of all classes at 2 p.m., and more than 1,000 students gathered on the Diag. Lathered up, they proceeded to march across South State Street to the new Administration Building. Four hundred students did not stop at the door, since it was not locked, and streamed right in. Half of them managed to squeeze into the very conference room where the Regents were meeting, while the rest clogged the outer offices and hallways. The Regents had already taken their vote on the bookstore, and stayed quiet as the invading students mostly lurked. After a few awkward moments the meeting recessed, the Regents agreeing to meet students in the nearby Michigan Union to announce and discuss their decision.

The Regents told the students that this time the bookstore proposal had carried. But before any great cheering could erupt they added their conditions: First, the plan must be approved by a new student referendum, this time to be conducted on a college-by-college, rather than campus-wide, basis. And second, the bookstore would not exactly be *run* by students. Administrators would be in charge, *advised* by a board that would include a few students. The "yes, but . . ." vote only made the students angrier.

A funny thing happened the next day, Saturday, September 20. Another crowd—ultimately many times larger than Friday's—began to gather, starting out as small groups of friends flowing purposely from the dorms and Greek houses and apartments and rooming houses, through the Diag, along the many campus walkways, down South U., Hill, State, and Main streets, multiplying in size and gaining strength until it flowed like a great human maize-and-blue river. Many of the same angry, shaggy-headed demonstrators and revolutionists who had crashed yesterday's Regents meeting were moving with it, some carrying placards of protest, or wearing American flags sewn upside down to their pant seats, or thrusting black-gloved fists in the air, or passing joints and bottles of Boones Farm. But also in the crowd were thousands of their parents and progenitors—old "M" grads, both recent and ancient, mostly clean-cut and well-dressed, a good many of them somewhere between baffled and bereaved over the anarchy that seemed to be consuming their beloved University.

Against all odds, 70,183 members of this crazy mix pretty much checked their political baggage at the turnstiles and united in spirit inside Michigan Stadium for the debut of the unknown Schembechler, expecting to be amused, partly by a football team no one expected much from, and the rest of the time by the intoxications of the late-summer sunshine, cannabis-infused breezes and slugs of apple wine, the traditional hands-to-hands overhead passing of willing "coeds" up the great bowl's 90 rows, and, of course, the thunder of 200 Marching Men of Michigan (there were not yet any Marching Women).

The Wolverines' 42–14 triumph over Vanderbilt turned out to be a pleasant diversion from the serious business at hand, which resumed immediately after the final gun, when 12,000 people massed outside the stadium and moved off on an organized peace march back to the Diag. "Six marchers bore a symbolic casket holding the corpse of Uncle Sam," the *Daily* reported. "On the casket was a Nixon poster bearing the message, 'Would you buy a used war from this man?'"

Two days later, 2,000 students massed outside ROTC headquarters at North Hall. Sixty of them stormed the building and barricaded themselves inside for the night. A force of 200 riot cops was mobilized at Ann Arbor police headquarters, but was not called into action. The ROTC occupiers decided to leave the building by a back door at 2:45 a.m. Tuesday. They were videotaped by surveillance cameras as they left, and Fleming vowed to "prosecute anyone we can identify."

Seething masses filled the Diag on Tuesday and Wednesday, fueled by the latest developments and Fleming's threat. On Thursday the 25th, the afternoon Diag rally became heated enough to send the crowd marching again to the Administration Building. This time they found the door locked. Someone broke a window. A delegation asked for a meeting with Fleming, and was denied. The angry crowd decided to move back to the LSA Building. Once there, several hundred students stormed into the lobby and planted themselves for a long occupation. At 6 p.m. Fleming entered the building and warned the student occupiers that the University was seeking a restraining order against them and that violators would be prosecuted. Some students decided to leave and join the much larger crowd that had been swelling outside on South State Street as the sit-in wore on. But more than 100 students remained inside. At 8:20 p.m. Fleming declared the building closed and ordered everyone out. At 10:30 p.m. Ann Arbor Police Chief Walter Krasny tried to enter the building to serve an injunction on the occupiers, but he was blocked by the crowd outside, now numbering more than 1,500. Meanwhile, Fleming decided to meet after all with some of the protest leaders, who told him they would end the sit-in if he called an emergency meeting of the Regents within 24 hours. But, one of the students who was present told the *Daily*, Fleming "was unwilling to participate. He refused to negotiate and after 10 minutes he walked out."

Around 3:30 a.m. a motorcade of yellow buses pulled up in front of the LSA Building, and out poured some 230 helmet-clad, riot-geared local and state police officers and county sheriff's deputies. Behind shields and swinging riot batons, they charged through the hundreds of students still holding vigil and blocking access to the students still occupying the building. Several students told the *Daily* that they had been made to "run a gauntlet" of officers who hit and poked them with sticks, and at least one student claimed to have been brutally beaten. When the siege ended around 5 a.m., 107 students had been arrested.

On Friday the 26th, SGC called a general student strike for Monday.

On Saturday the 27th, the Wolverines demolished Washington, 45–7—before an extremely meager stadium crowd of 49,684.

The Monday strike fizzled, as students were apparently more exhausted and shell-shocked than ready for more trouble. Leaders regrouped and set two new action targets: the nationwide Moratorium to end the war two weeks out, and the next on-campus meeting of the Regents, two days after that.

On Wednesday, October 15, more than a million Americans opposed to the war in Vietnam joined demonstrations in Washington and every major city and college campus in the country. The *Daily* reported that classes at the University—officially operating as usual—were mostly vacant in the schools of LSA, Social Work, Education, and Music, while attendance in Engineering, Business Administration, and Natural Resources was near normal. As 20,000 anti-war demonstrators gathered for a massive Moratorium rally inside the stadium (surrounded by 80,000 empty seats), Schembechler, whose team was now 3–1 after losing to Missouri but beating Purdue, was in his office explaining to the *Daily* that the bulk of *his* concerns were with Saturday's road game at Michigan State: "We're preparing to *wage* a war, not end one," Bo said with a wink.

Friday, October 17, was a great day of triumph for Michigan students. The Regents, sensing a problem that would otherwise never go away, finally approved the establishment of a bookstore to be controlled by a student-dominated board.

Saturday, October 18, was *not* a great day. Michigan lost to archrival Michigan State, 23–12.

After that, however, things took a good turn. On November 11, students capped their bookstore victory by overwhelmingly voting themselves a whopping $5-per-head assessment to fund the business. On the 19th, the Faculty Senate voted overwhelmingly to recommend that the University give ROTC the boot.

Meanwhile, the Wolverines bounced back from the MSU loss and suddenly turned into a doomsday machine, rolling over Minnesota, Wisconsin, Illinois, and Iowa by a combined score of 178–22. It was looking like Bo's war was one the students could not get enough of.

All that remained now was the true test, the season's final game—perhaps—against what more experts than ever were calling the greatest college football team ever assembled. Ohio State was looking to finish a second consecutive perfect season by making Michigan its 23rd-straight victim. The small solace for Wolverine fans was that no matter what happened on November 22, the Wolverines had an excellent chance of being chosen to represent the Big Ten in the 1970 Rose Bowl—if only because the conference barred its teams from playing in Pasadena two years in a row. But such a reward following another loss to the hated Buckeyes would be a hollow one, indeed. And sure enough, in the days leading up to the showdown between Bo and his plus-sized mentor, the sports pages and airwaves from coast to coast were filled with presumptive regrets and apologies that America's greatest team would not be allowed to sanctify its eminence in a repeat romp in the Granddaddy of all the bowls.

Maybe nobody in the crowd of 103,588 saw it coming but Bo. Somehow it figured that Ann Arbor's wild and wrenching Fall of '69 would be capped by the greatest upset in college football history, in front of the largest crowd of students and fans ever to fill Michigan Stadium to that point. Bo's ball-control offense struck for three touchdowns in the first half—two by pile-driving fullback Garvie Craw and one by quarterback Don Moorhead—while the defense totally shut down the vaunted Buckeye scoring machine, intercepting six passes, four of them against All-America quarterback Rex Kern. A 24–12 Michigan lead at halftime became the delirious final score after neither team put up a point in the final 30 minutes.

It's fair to say that the bookstore wars, ROTC fights, racial struggles, anti-authority uprisings, anger, distrust, and general disillusionment were forgotten for a few hours on November 22, 1969—or at least moved to a back burner until after the all-night, all-weekend, all-consuming partying would wind down. On the sixth anniversary of the darkest day when Americans witnessed the murder of their president, and just 11 weeks into the University of Michigan's worst year ever, everything was coming up Roses.

Post Script:

Just a few hours before the Rose Bowl on the morning of January 1, 1970, 40-year-old Bo Schembechler suffered a heart attack and was admitted into a Pasadena hospital. He was not allowed to watch the game on television, which was a good thing, because the Wolverines lost to Southern Cal, 10–3.

On March 19, 1970, another violent confrontation between students and police erupted on campus, this time involving members and supporters of the Black Action Movement, who were demanding an increase in African-American enrollment. BAM's call for a general strike drew strong campus-wide support, and the University was effectively shut down for 12 days, ultimately forcing the Regents to commit to, and fully fund, a plan to increase black enrollment to 10 percent by 1973–74.

On April 30, President Nixon announced a massive invasion of Cambodia, vastly expanding the war in Southeast Asia. Almost immediately student protests broke out all across the country. On Monday, May 4, Ohio national guardsmen mobilized by the governor to quell protests at Kent State, opened fire on a group of students, killing four and leaving nine others wounded.

More than 450 college campuses immediately shut down, leaving hundreds of thousands of students to close out the tragic academic year of 1969–70 without final exams and, in many cases, final grades.

The University of Michigan was not among them.

Thanks to the quirks of the trimester system, Michigan students had already completed their finals by the time of Nixon's announcement.

Most of them had left town.

John Papanek joined the *Michigan Daily* in 1970 and served as sports editor from 1972 to 1973. Seven months after graduation he was hired as a reporter at *Sports Illustrated*, where he worked his way up to staff writer, then senior editor, and in 1988 became the founding editor of *Sports Illustrated Kids*. Two years later he returned to *SI* as the youngest chief editor in the magazine's history, racking up several National Magazine Awards in his tenure. In 1997 Papanek became *SI*'s chief competitor in creating and editing *ESPN The Magazine,* securing another bundle of awards. He went on to develop and lead the groundbreaking ESPN.com and serve the company as a senior vice president until his retirement in 2011. He continues to write on a variety of subjects while making good on a lifelong dream of being a jazz saxophonist.

"NO WOMEN" WAS NO BARRIER

SARA KRULWICH

September 20, 1969

Fall meant football at the University of Michigan, but the photo department at the *Michigan Daily*, where I worked as its first woman photographer, was given only four press passes. As a freshman, I was not entitled to one. Seniority was not the only problem. In 1968, the passes all said, "No women, children or dogs allowed on the field." This was no joke. There were no women in the marching band; no women cheerleaders; no women security guards. A year later, I earned one of the coveted passes. The rules had loosened a bit. The new passes said, "No women or children allowed on the field."

Dogs were now allowed.

On the first day of the season, Andy Sacks, a former *Daily* photographer who was covering the game for UPI, agreed to introduce me to the director of sports information, Will Perry. He was sitting in the press box overlooking the stadium. Andy said I worked for the *Daily* and should be allowed to cover the game. Mr. Perry just looked at us and said he couldn't make the decision right then.

We left and made our way down from the press box right onto the field. Three guards surrounded me and asked what I was doing. I said I had talked to Will Perry. I didn't tell them what Mr. Perry had said, but they found out soon enough. They told me to leave the field or they would have to physically remove me. When I asked why, they pointed to the part of my pass that said "No women."

"Can't you read?" they asked. I assured them I could, but explained as

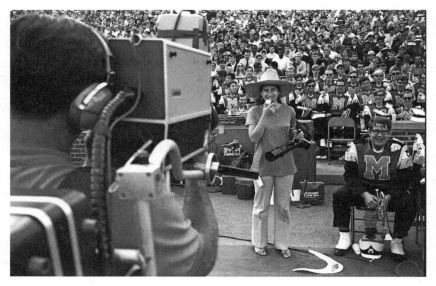

Photo by Jay Cassidy.

calmly as possible that I didn't understand why women weren't allowed on the field. I told them I had a right to be there and finished by saying that I could shoot pictures as well as anyone else on the field. They said they would give me a few minutes to decide whether to leave voluntarily or to be dragged off the field.

I asked my friends to stay around to document whatever was going to happen, gathered up my courage and—with tears in my eyes—told them that they would have to physically remove me.

Right at that moment, the game began. Andy told me just kneel down and start shooting. (The seats in Michigan's stadium are at field level, so photographers had to kneel to avoid obstructing views.) If the guards had tried to remove me, they would have blocked the views of front-row fans and had 100,000 more people as witnesses. They decided to let me shoot. That is how I became the first woman on the football field at the University of Michigan.

A few days later, Mr. Perry wrote a letter of apology. I still have it hanging on my wall. "I guess the generation gap and 12 years of sports writing with only men around have begun to set in and determine the thoughts," he began. He said he had checked with the sports editor and found out that I was "a regular photo gal." He concluded: "Sorry for any dogmatic approach I may have taken. Hope you get some fine pictures. I would like to have one some time to keep from our 'first' woman photographer."

Ten years later I returned to Michigan to cover a game as a staff photographer for the *New York Times*. The sidelines looked totally different. There were women cheerleaders, women in the band, women in the security force, women physical therapists and a woman photographer who happened to be the photo editor at the *Michigan Daily*. By then, no one could even imagine it otherwise.

My first act of civil disobedience remains one of the most important days of my life. It was the moment that convinced me to make photojournalism my career. I learned that it takes a certain kind of personality to risk arrest on your 19th birthday in front of 100,000 people in order to shoot a photo assignment. I also learned that if you turn out to be that kind of person, being a newspaper photographer is the best job in the world.

This story originally ran on the New York Times Lens blog on May 22, 2009. It is printed with permission from the Times.

Sara Krulwich was a photographer at the *Michigan Daily* from 1968 to 1972. Finding a newspaper job after graduation was a challenge. The photo editor at the *Hartford Courant* put it this way: "Why would I hire a woman? It would be like hiring half a photographer. We could never send you to a bad neighborhood. You couldn't be the last one on at night, and we would have to change our language around you." After hunting for a newspaper job for almost a year, she found one at the *Providence Journal* as its first woman photographer. She then moved on to work in Connecticut as the *Journal Inquirer*'s first woman photographer. After about two years, she became the chief photographer of a staff of four. In 1976, she was hired by the *Philadelphia Inquirer* and again was a trailblazer as its first woman photographer. She worked there for almost three years, until she left to work at the *New York Times*, where she has remained for 36 years. Krulwich was a general assignment photographer for her first 15 years and a dedicated culture photographer for over the last 20 years. Theater photography has become her specialty. She shoots over one hundred shows a year.

THE DAY PAUL WAS PROCLAIMED DEAD

LESLIE WAYNE

October 14, 1969

Hard to imagine that a story that was entirely untrue brought worldwide fame to the *Michigan Daily*. But it did.

"McCartney dead; new evidence brought to light" said the headline. And, on October 14, 1969, that page two *Daily* story spread like wildfire across the globe. Clues pointing to Paul's death, three years earlier in a car accident, were sprinkled through Beatles music, photos, and album covers, and a grand conspiracy with a fake McCartney had taken place, so said the *Daily*.

In a breathless "now it can be told" tone, Paul's death and the ensuing cover-up were laid out in rich detail—and the world took notice. All the various signs of his death outlined in the *Daily*—Paul walking barefoot on the cover of the Abbey Road album; turning his back on the album cover of Sgt. Pepper's Lonely Hearts Club Band—were being dissected from Hollywood to London and beyond. Was it true? Was it not? No one really knew.

The story revealed a tragic end for the popular Beatle: In November 1966, Paul was killed in his Aston Martin after leaving the EMI recording studio "tired, sad, and dejected." Four hours later, he was found "pinned under his car in a culvert with the top of his head sheared off. He was deader than a doornail."

A reader may ask why a student newspaper in Ann Arbor was breaking this news to the world. And, why was the copy on page two and not a banner headline on the front? All are good questions. And here's how it happened.

I like to think that had I come to work at the *Daily* that October night, rumors of Paul's demise might have just remained idle chatter and fame would have passed over the *Daily*. So it's good I stayed away. My absence allowed the story to appear. I was the managing arts editor, in charge of posting movie and music reviews, and stories about the arts on the *Daily*'s page two. My deputy was the late, great John Gray, and he was accompanied by his sidekick Fred LaBour, who now, decades later, is keeping the singing cowboy tradition alive as a member of the Grammy-awarding winning musical group Riders in the Sky. (Fred also goes by the stage name of "Two Slim.")

That October night, John and Fred were left in charge of the page, and I had given them the usual mix of copy—can't remember exactly what—to edit and post. That's not what they did, of course. Fred had listened to a radio call-in show the night before that discussed rumors circulating in London and in America about Paul's death in a car crash. This came after a real fender bender involving Paul's car. Fred and John ignored the copy I had given them. Instead, putting paper into typewriter, they devised a mash-up of symbols, innuendo, falsehoods, outrageous lies, and a complicated conspiracy theory about Paul's passing. It was brilliant.

Dripping with earnestness and satire, Fred and John's story revealed the hidden tale. It wasn't the first or only story to traffic in these rumors. Yet it was the most clever, and it caught fire. Fred and John put an elegant black box around an artful photo of Paul and captioned it O.P.D. 1966— or "Officially Pronounced Dead." Then came the clues, each one more plausible, mysterious, and captivating than the next. An orphan from Edinburgh named William Campbell, with some minor plastic surgery, was brought in as a fake Paul so that the world would never know: "Campbell nearly erased entirely his own speech patterns and successfully adopted the late McCartney's." John Lennon, suffering from a God complex, wanted to turn the late Paul into a Messiah and concocted a cover-up that, the *Daily* said, "took on terrifying proportions."

Even so, signs of Paul's death were everywhere if you just looked. Play "Strawberry Fields Forever" at a slow 45 r.p.m., and there's a "distorted voice saying, 'I buried Paul.'" More telling was that if anyone played "I am the Walrus" backwards, "the words 'Paul is dead' can be plainly heard," according to the story. Across the country, that's just what people did, by the thousands. Perhaps a hint that Fred was engaging in make-believe might come from a sentence earlier in that paragraph saying that "'Walrus' is Greek for corpse"—which it is not.

My favorite passages are the ones that delve into the symbolism on the famous Abbey Road album cover. Any summary would not do it justice, so here's the original copy:

"Thus we come to Abbey Road (Monks live in abbeys). On the cover is John Lennon, dressed in white and resembling utterly an anthropomorphic God, followed by Ringo the undertaker, followed by Paul the resurrected, barefoot with a cigarette in his right hand (the original was left handed), followed by George, the grave digger.

And if you look closely, they have just walked out of a cemetery on the left side of the street. Thus, Paul was resurrected, given a cigarette, and led out of the tomb, thereby conquering death with a little help from his friends.

The real Paul is dead, of course, but his symbolic resurrection works fine without him."

A hoax doesn't get much better than that. I didn't know about the Paul-is-dead story until the next day when I picked up my *Michigan Daily* and saw what John and Fred had done. Honestly, I didn't know how to feel, what to make of it all—or what happened to the copy I had given them. The ensuing storm of attention over the piece quickly made it apparent that something special had just taken place. Fred was flown to Hollywood to discuss it on television. Radio stations around the country, and the world, debated it on air. The Beatles debunked it. The frenzy lasted for weeks until *Life* magazine—the most popular in the country—published a cover story with Paul's photo and headlined "Paul is still with us."

A lot happened that year, 1969, some good, and a lot, bad. Americans landed on the moon. Joan Baez and a galaxy of musical stars came to Ann Arbor. There was the draft lottery that could send you to war based on the luck, or unluck, of a draw, and protests galore over Vietnam, civil rights, and so much else. A naked troupe of performers, called the Living Theater, performed "Dionysus in '69." It was a year of high drama when so much seemed important, grim, or transformative.

That's why I'm glad Fred and John snuck "Paul is Dead" in the paper. It provided a lively distraction and set off a global scavenger hunt that put all things Beatles under a microscope. It was clever and a bit absurd. It was cheeky and fun to read. Even more, I'm glad it wasn't true.

Leslie Wayne was a reporter and managing arts editor at the *Michigan Daily* from 1967 to 1970. After graduation, she joined the *News & Observer* in Raleigh, North Carolina, where she covered politics, and then moved on to the *Philadelphia Inquirer*. While at the *Daily*, she also was the campus stringer for the *New York Times*, and later joined the *Times* in 1981, covering business and politics, until 2010. Along the way, she picked up an MBA from Columbia University and various journalism awards. She continues to write for the *Times* as a contributor and teaches business journalism at both Columbia and New York University.

A TIME FOR TEMPO HEAVY CONDENSED

SARA FITZGERALD

January 22, 1973

It was, the *Michigan Daily* noted, "a cold rainy day in Ann Arbor." The night before, I had driven a Ford Maverick filled with members of what we brashly called "The *Michigan Daily* Washington Bureau" back from a weekend trip to cover Richard M. Nixon's second inauguration. Fifty thousand demonstrators had turned out to protest the war in Vietnam, but the steam seemed to be running out of the anti-war movement. With just a few days left of my term as editor-in-chief of the *Daily*, I knew my energies were running out, too.

The news broke over the wire machines in the morning, when the *Daily* newsroom was usually at its emptiest: In a 7–2 decision, the U.S. Supreme Court had ruled that states could not restrict a woman's right to an abortion in the first 12 weeks of a pregnancy. *Roe v. Wade* had been written into the history books.

Before that morning, prospects for change had been discouraging. The previous November, Michigan voters had rejected—by a 3 to 2 margin—a referendum to make abortion legal in the state in the first 20 weeks of pregnancy. In more than 30 states, including Michigan, it was still a crime to perform an abortion except to save the life of the mother. The Supreme Court's ruling amounted to a stunning, unexpected victory for women's rights advocates, particularly coming from a court in which Nixon appointees were in the majority and on which a woman had still never served. It was, in the words of the *Daily*'s editorial on the decision, "almost too good to be true."

For me, the decision was also personal. Just five months before, I had joined the ranks of women who traveled to New York during that era to obtain an abortion. Most of my *Daily* colleagues did not know that I was the anonymous author of a lengthy story about my experience, published a few weeks after my return.

The morning announcement of the high court's decision provided more than enough time to get our coverage in place. The main story was combined from three wire services. (Thanks to the Wolverines' trip to the 1972 Rose Bowl—in the days when that was the only bowl game possible—the *Daily*'s advertising revenues had surged enough to support the addition of Reuters.) A sidebar detailing the local reaction and impact was assigned to Jan Benedetti, a senior who covered women's issues. Finally, someone began drafting the editorial that the senior editors would sign.

Everyone recognized that this was a very big story; the only discussion was over "how big." As the sun went down and the staff gathered for that day's news conference, the consensus was that this was an occasion worthy of the "Tempo Heavy Condensed" (a.k.a. THC) headline type that was an option for the *Daily*'s hot-metal presses. Thick, dark, all-caps, and charmingly old-fashioned. In my memory, the initial decision was for an eight-column headline, probably with two lines.

The meeting was breaking up when the bells on the wire machine rang again. (Perhaps the years have added the bells to my memories.) In any case, a junior member of the staff broke the news off the wires: Former President Lyndon B. Johnson had died of a heart attack. We were back to square one—now with two sharply divergent points of view on which story should be the lead.

One side, dominated by male members of the staff, argued that Johnson's role as the chief arbiter of the Vietnam War justified giving his death the more prominent play. While Johnson had had health concerns over the years, his death was nevertheless sudden and unexpected. (Many years later, I learned that Walter Cronkite had actually accepted a phone call from Tom Johnson, the president's longtime press aide, in the middle of his nightly newscast to report the breaking story.)

The other side, dominated by female members of the staff, argued that as important as Johnson had been to the defining event of our generation, he was, after all, a *former* president. Four years had passed since he had been in office. He no longer had any impact on the course of the war or our lives. The Supreme Court's decision, on the other hand, amounted to a revolutionary development, granting rights that would enable women for the first time to control their own bodies and thus their futures. The impact of the court's decision, we believed, would reverberate for many years to come.

If there was a time when that decision was the editor-in-chief's to make, that time had passed. The societal changes of the late 1960's and early 1970's had their impact on the *Daily*, too. It was, to my knowledge, the beginning of a trend toward greater democracy on the paper (for better or for worse). In recent years, the editor-in-chief had been chosen by the outgoing senior editors. I had been selected by a vote of my senior editor peers, after the editor-in-chief resigned midway through his year. The class after mine informed us that they intended to pick their own editors, and installed two talented friends, Eugene Robinson and Chris Parks, as co-editors. (Gene went on to become a Pulitzer Prize–winning columnist for the *Washington Post*, and Chris became Lansing bureau chief for UPI.)

The month before our Johnson versus *Roe v. Wade* debate, I had tried to assess the paper's accomplishments in a journal I kept at the time: "Institutionally," I wrote, "the *Daily* is somewhat more democratic this year. The Senior Editor box is alphabetized. We've had more staff meetings (indeed, we're afraid to do anything without approval—in fact, the editor is virtually unable to do anything without senior editor approval). News conferences aren't torturous (of course, layouts are often repetitious)."

That night's news conference was apparently an exception, which is probably why I remember it to this day. I'm not sure how we decided who got to vote. The "News Staff" for that day's paper listed seven women, including the managing editor and an assistant managing editor. Perhaps all you needed to do to earn a vote was to show up and stay late. Pat Bauer, the associate managing editor working that night, recalls that Gene and Chris, the incoming co-editors, ultimately carried the day by arguing that their time had come, and that their view should prevail.

However the debate played out, my side lost. The Johnson headline went on top, with one line of 96-point type, across eight columns. *Roe v. Wade* still got THC treatment, but only across seven columns and lower on the page. In retrospect, journalistic observers might actually disagree which story was given the most prominent display. But I knew which side had won.

The next day, I received a note from Joel Berger, a *Daily* alum who was then one of the top-ranking people in the University's public relations shop. Joel commended the job we had done covering both stories, including the

ABORTION
REFORM AT LAST
See Editorial Page

INEXCUSABLE
High—58
Low—39
See today . . . for details

The Michigan Daily

Vol. LXXXIII, No. 99   Ann Arbor, Michigan—Tuesday, January 23, 1973   Ten Cents   Eight Pages

LBJ dies of heart attack at 64

JOHNSON CONFERS with South Vietnam's then-Premier Nguyen Cao Ky (left), Henry Cabot Lodge (back, right) and then-Defense Secretary Robert McNamara (back, left) in a February, 1966, meeting in Honolulu.

NATIONWIDE ABORTION MADE LEGAL
IN SURPRISE SUPREME COURT RULING

today . . .
If you see news happen call 76-DAILY

Berrigans restricted

Goodbye, dual world

Security leak

Happenings . . .

On the inside

The weather picture

The new 'champeen'

George Foreman (left) crashes crushing blow to Joe Frazier as the young challenger stopped Frazier in the second round to win the heavyweight championship of the world (See story, Page 7).

DOCTOR'S OK REQUIRED;
THREE-MONTH LIMIT SET

See related story, Page 9

KISSINGER IN PARIS:

Peace agreement may be signed by weekend

JOHNSON TELLS the University community about his "Great Society," as he receives an honorary doctorate in May, 1964.

COLD SNAP FEARED

Fuel shortage threatens the 'U'

See related story, Page 1

Statesmen and public mourn LBJ's death

By PAUL TRAVIS

See LBJ, Page 8

Courtesy of Sara Fitzgerald.

sidebar of local reaction to Johnson's death that associate managing editor Paul Travis had produced on deadline and the use of a photo of Johnson speaking at the University of Michigan's 1964 commencement (when he first envisioned his "Great Society"). I appreciated that Joel had taken the time to send a note, but his praise for the page only made me feel worse.

Several years later, I met Sarah Weddington, who as a young Texas lawyer had argued the abortion case before the court and later served in the Carter White House. I told her the story about our debate, and learned that she had begun collecting copies of newspapers' coverage of the decision. Although my arguments had failed to carry the day, I was still proud of our big, bold headline and made a copy of the page to send to her. I observed that the *Daily* was probably one of the few newspapers in the country that had correctly understood not only the immediate impact of that decision but how important it would continue to be. She agreed.

Recently, I looked back to compare our newsplay decision to that of three major American papers. All of them played Johnson's death as the lead. The *New York Times*' headlines were closest to the *Daily*'s—eight columns for both stories. The *Washington Post* relegated the abortion decision to a three-column headline. The *Los Angeles Times*, meanwhile, gave it one-column play, placed below a feature on Canadian immigration policy, a volcanic eruption in Iceland, and George Foreman's defeat of Joe Frazier for the world heavyweight boxing title.

In January 2013, the 40th anniversary of the court's decision provided me with the opportunity to recall that night on The Michigan Daily Alumni's Facebook page. My own memories have softened over the years, and some of that night's once-bitter combatants went on to become very close friends.

Some of those who were there still continue to argue that they were right. But staff member Judy Ruskin, the widow of Chris Parks, observed in a post that her late husband, "who was firmly in the LBJ camp, later admitted he was wrong because in the end LBJ was just another dead white guy."

And I smiled to learn that more junior staff members also remembered that night. Stephen Selbst, who briefly worked as a reporter before becoming a lawyer and, for six years, a member of the University's Board for Student Publications, recalled: "My first night as a trainee on the night desk. Huge news and the senior editors (also known as gods on earth) are having this spirited discussion about which story will run lead.

"Hooked from that moment on."

Sara Fitzgerald began working at the *Michigan Daily* in 1970. She served as editor-in-chief from 1972 to 1973 and is believed to be the first woman to have held that post. Over the course of her career in journalism, she worked for the *Washington Post*, *National Journal* magazine, and the *St. Petersburg Times*. The *Daily* article she wrote about her abortion won the grand prize in the 1973 Detroit Press Club Foundation competition and a Sigma Delta Chi Mark of Excellence Award that same year.

"HIS POETRY, MY PROSE"

LAURA BERMAN

February 2, 1975

Donald Hall was the English department's literary star, a working poet with a Harvard and Oxford pedigree. Shaggy-haired and charismatic, he was also a figure of intrigue—a professor who had, it was said, recently married one of his graduate students. In an interview in his Hopwood Room office, he was frank about poetry as a seductive art form: "I first started writing poetry to get attention, to be loved by women," he said, as my tape recorder whirred.

Hall was a celebrated writer with a capital W, who had a play in the works, readying for production on campus. And the writer ideal loomed large among the members of our tiny *Sunday Magazine* staff in 1975.

As co-editor of the *Michigan Daily's Sunday Magazine* that semester, along with Dan Borus, I had sent myself out to profile Ann Arbor's most celebrated resident poet, in part because getting close to a real Writer seemed like one way to get closer to becoming one.

The magazine was then a two-year-old fledgling effort, founded the year before by Tony Schwartz and Martin Porter. As a team, they were a classic odd couple in appearance—Tony, lanky and dynamic; Marty, bear-sized and accompanied by various dogs—but they were both ambitious, funny, and impatient with traditions, even sacrosanct *Daily* traditions.

Their immodest goal in the fall of 1973 was to give readers the equivalent of then cutting-edge *New York Magazine* within the confines of a weekly *Michigan Daily* insert. Gay Talese, Tom Wolfe, Nora Ephron—journalists who toyed with fictional techniques, inserted themselves into the story, or pushed journalistic convention in other ways—were inspirations. Responding to Tony's note on the *Daily* bulletin board, I signed up immediately.

By the time I set off to profile Donald Hall and his play, "Bread and Roses," in 1975, he was immersed in last-minute script excisions and rehearsals, trying to capture the drama of the early American labor movement group, the so-called "Wobblies," and their larger-than-life leaders, from Joe Hill to Big Bill Haywood. That day at the Power Center, he was fretting about the scene and student actors who were "making this song about oppressed workers sound like a Michigan football cheer."

At 21, I was in love with the idea of writing, even if the actual work of it was daunting. Here was a well-known poet who was willing to ruminate, pontificate, and explain the work of it as a career. Hall encouraged the belief that sitting alone in a room with only words for company was a gift, and striving to write a great poem was the calling he had accepted, whether attainable or not.

He was gracious and engaging and improbably seductive. "I like varying the rhythms of sentences . . . I love to play with them, fool with them, get my hands into them," he said, in a voice as lyrical as his words.

At the time, he was taking solace in prose—profiles for the *New Yorker*, this play—because poetry wasn't going well. He was frank about this: "It's like sex or something you take fantastic joy in, so you can't imagine life without it. And when there comes a time when you can't do it, you're miserable."

That confirmed some of the rumors I'd heard. A *Daily* colleague, a senior, had bluntly told me that Hall's best work was behind him. Hall was getting older, the friend said—(he was in fact 46), the play would never move beyond the Power Center, and the professor hadn't published or won a major award in years.

While these harsh judgments do not appear in the *Sunday Magazine* profile, titled "Poet Donald Hall: For now, at least, the play's the thing," that appeared February 2, 1975, they echoed in my head, as I pecked into the night on my portable electric typewriter.

At the time, I was striving for sophistication and perspective on the writer's life. Was his career mostly over? I wondered. Wasn't his new wife, the young poet who had so rashly married this charming but older man, in for it? Surely, she would soon be his caretaker or, worse, a young widow. Was this to be his life, teaching poetry until retirement, chasing after the elusive great poem that never comes?

Hall described in our interview, with candor, his belief in writing as a lifelong love requiring unwavering devotion. But it was so many years later, in the poetic arc of his well-documented life, that I appreciated Hall's lesson of that day.

A few months after the *Michigan Daily* profile appeared, the poet couple decamped from Ann Arbor, moving to Hall's great-grandfather's farm at Eagle Pond in New Hampshire. His wife, the former graduate student 19 years younger, became the brilliant and renowned poet Jane Kenyon. At Eagle Pond Farm, they each wrote every day, in separate rooms, creating poetry from the mundane and beautiful world around them.

Some of what I imagined as an all-knowing college journalist came true: Hall got colon cancer, while his younger wife remained at his side. When the cancer eventually attacked his liver and he underwent surgery to remove the cancerous portion, they returned home together, anticipating an ending.

"I was thinking my time was probably short. It didn't happen that way," the still-eloquent Hall said in a videotaped interview decades later, recorded by the online site Web of Stories. "It happened otherwise."

The "otherwise" was Jane Kenyon's diagnosis with leukemia, the disease that killed her 15 months later in 1995, just short of her 48th birthday. Hall became the widower, not Kenyon. In his poem "Affirmation," he wrote sardonically of his life's unfolding: "If a new love carries us / past middle age / our wife will die / at her strongest and most beautiful."

Despite *Michigan Daily* staff predictions, Hall did not fade into obscurity. In 2006, he was named the 14th U.S. Poet Laureate. As I write these words, he is 86, still working, still seeking precise combinations of words to illuminate the experience of being alive in the world. His latest book, "Essays After Eighty," was published in December 2014. At 21, as a striving sophisticate alone with a typewriter, I imagined the ways his life might devolve. Now, decades later, I am still learning from the unexpected trajectory of my former *Sunday Magazine* subject's long life. Sometimes, love between a man and a woman—even a much younger woman—and high ideals about the sanctity of writing turn out to be worthy and true, a life's saving grace.

Laura Berman joined the *Michigan Daily* immediately upon arriving in Ann Arbor in 1972, working as a reporter, news editor, and in 1974–1975, co-editor of the *Sunday Magazine*. After graduation, she was hired by the *Detroit Free*

Press, writing about everything but sports. In the past two decades, she has been an award-winning columnist at the *Detroit News*, where she has covered Bill Clinton's impeachment, the aftermath of the Bosnian war, and Detroit's long, winding road to bankruptcy. Her work has appeared in *Newsweek*, *Fortune*, *Time*, and other national magazines.

SO DID YOU KNOW BO?

BILL STIEG

January 1977

Bo looked me in the eye.

"Let me tell you something," he said.

I nodded and glanced down at my notebook. When Bo Schembechler looked you in the eye, it was difficult—disrespectful, it seemed—to look away. But I was still writing down his previous sentences. I could never scribble fast enough to capture the crisp cadence of his speech, that jabbing staccato that held reporters, players, alumni—anyone within earshot, let alone eye-lock—spellbound.

I really could've used a digital recorder, or an iPhone. But this was 1977.

It was a dead-quiet winter weekday afternoon in his office at the end of a hallway in the Athletic Department at State and Hoover, just the two of us. Frankly, I was a surprised to be sitting there.

Bo didn't really know me. I can't say that I really knew Bo, though I'm sure I've allowed that impression to float unchallenged at a few dinner parties since my years at Michigan. I covered the team my senior year; to him, I was just one of the guys from the *Daily*. I doubt that he knew my name.

A few days earlier we had both been in Pasadena, where Michigan had lost to Southern California in the Rose Bowl. I watched from the press box as Rick Leach led the team to the USC 17-yard line in the closing minutes before throwing two incompletions. Bo of course watched from the sidelines, squinting and snarling.

It was Schembechler's third Rose Bowl loss in his eight seasons at Michigan, to go with an Orange Bowl loss the previous year. He was 0–7–1 in season-ending games. Michigan, which had won 10 regular-season games by an average score of 41–7, managed one touchdown against Southern Cal, the Los Angeles team that was playing its eighth Rose Bowl in the past 11 years.

It was practically a home game for the Trojans, Bo was telling me as I scrawled and flipped pages. The USC quarterback had had "a helluva day. He had *the* day." The Rose Bowl was natural turf, Bo reminded me, not the fast carpet the Michigan option offense was used to sprinting across. "I'd like to see them come out here for two weeks to prepare to play us in Michigan Stadium," he said. The conjecture carried no trace of bitterness—more thought experiment than excuse.

In five months of covering the team, I'd interviewed Bo one-on-one just a handful of times, usually on a Tuesday or Wednesday evening after practice. He'd come to the door of the coaches' locker room, friendly and jokey, and give me something—an injury update, a team-mood check, an observation about the upcoming game. Innocuous fodder for advance stories. Usually it would only be me or one of the other *Daily* seniors—Rich Lerner, Andy Glazer, or Rick Bonino. During a big week, maybe someone from the *Ann Arbor News* or The Associated Press would wait by the door with us.

We *Daily* staffers spent much more time talking to players—our classmates, really. They were, to begin with, more approachable than Bo. And I had unusual access. As sports editor, I was a member of Michigamua, that once notorious (harmless, really) not-so-secret society that was mostly a drinking club and alumni network. Through the group, I came to know several players, and they encouraged teammates to talk to me.

This was all part of the odd dance we did as students covering fellow students who happened to play games for a lucrative quasi-business run by serious adults (hello, Mr. Canham) and tough coaches accustomed to exerting control.

Back at 420 Maynard, the relatively hard-ass edit staffers of this Woodward-and-Bernstein era probably would have frowned on the fraternization we sports staffers engaged in—if they had known about it. In smoky hotel rooms with the basketball team (sorry, NCAA; the statute of limitations has expired) and over Village Bell pitchers with the Michigamua guys, we tirelessly gathered information. Yeah, that was it—just cultivating sources.

And yes, edit staffers, this probably led to some sympathizing with players, and some bias. But it also meant an invaluable course in big-time college football. My first lesson came after the opening game of the '76 season, a 40–27 win over Wisconsin. Impressive, right? Not really, not back then, and definitely not to Bo. *Twenty-seven points?* Unacceptable!

The day after that game, I was with a couple of players who were quietly discussing some of the defensive calls made by the coaches, which had left them out of position on Wisconsin's scores. I was scarcely aware that defenses had calls, let alone understood the terminology they were using. I was rapt. Not holding a notebook, I noticed, really changed things.

The next day was the weekly luncheon with Bo, a gathering of a dozen or so reporters in a hotel dining room. These were fun; we seniors took turns going. Bo would be relaxed and amusing. He'd eat quickly and then push back to answer our questions while we scribbled between bites of grilled chicken. At one point, after Bo had grumbled about the poor pursuit and tackling and the points allowed—more than in any game since his first season—I piped up.

"Is it possible," I ventured, "that some of the problems were caused by wrong defensive calls by the coaches?" I don't think my voice cracked.

Bo stared at me. Then he quickly agreed: "Absolutely. Absolutely." He went on to say there was plenty of blame to go around, from the coaches on down, for the lack of focus and execution, but I barely heard him. Bo Schembechler had validated my question! I like to think that he briefly wondered, *What does this kid know about defensive calls?*

(This sounds quaint, I know. Nowadays, with every game televised and DVR'd and analyzed, there is more technical insight in a single MGoBlog post than in my entire season's coverage. Times were different.)

That season unfolded majestically, with a No. 1 ranking and big win after big win. There was nothing even close, until there actually was a close game, at Purdue in November, and Michigan lost. I hadn't bothered to go—c'mon, Purdue?—and listened on the radio, pacing around my South Forest Avenue apartment, and finally slumping onto the couch.

Oh, the anguish this loss stirred. Sportswriters (including some on the *Daily*), students, and fans yelped: *See? Bo's ground offense can be stopped, and the team can't pass when it needs to.* There were no bloggers or talk radio back then, but the complaining was plenty loud. In truth, the reasons for the loss were more specific than systemic: fumbles, a dropped touchdown pass, and—*unacceptable!*—poor tackling on defense.

I'll admit I was inclined to defend the players and coaches, but not because I was friendly with one of the fumblers and three of the tacklers. The coaches' game plan and play calls racked up more than enough yardage to win. The players were human.

Moreover, my sympathy stemmed from a lifetime of going to Michigan Stadium, from kindergarten to freshman year in South Quad and beyond. In the 60's, during the off-season, my brother and I used to sneak into—actually, stroll right into—the stadium (a 10-minute walk from our grandmother's house) to play touch football. It was especially fun in the snow.

During the season, my brother, sister, and I would sit in the mostly-empty end zone as the team won some and lost almost as many. The Wolverines were 51–42–2 in those childhood years with Bump Elliott as coach. Their 1964 championship season and Rose Bowl victory was literally the thrill of a lifetime for a giddy 9-year-old me. Even on a black-and-white TV. My parents had painted a cheap plastic blue helmet with the maize stripes and wings that we kids could wear in the backyard. My brother, sister, and I represented the third generation of our family to attend the University; our parents met there, in speech class.

So yeah, I was a fan—like probably 95 percent of the sports staff—when I enrolled at Michigan in 1973 and signed up for the *Daily*. By then, Bo had spoiled us all. The 1969 upset, the routine routs, the two Rose Bowls in his first three years.

Freshman year, I sat in the end zone beside my best friend, Kevin Kennedy, with a perfect view as Mike Lantry's two late field goal attempts sailed wide, and the epic struggle with Ohio State ended in a 10–10 tie, and a tie for the Big Ten championship. I was exhausted. But also thrilled, because it meant, I assumed, that Michigan was headed to the Rose Bowl. (Kevin wasn't so sure.) Ohio State had gone the year before, and until that year the Big Ten had a rule never to send a team twice in a row. Besides, Michigan had almost won. Maybe Kevin and I could make it a road trip.

This was going to be great.

Then came The Vote. I don't remember where I was when news spread that the Big Ten athletic directors had voted to ignore decades of tradition to award that lone bowl berth to Ohio State. But I remember entering the Sunday night meeting of the shell-shocked sports staff and seeing Rich Stuck, a senior staffer who also worked as a student football manager (conflict much?) dejectedly toss a nickel-Coke bottle up toward that vaulted ceiling. We all watched it plummet, only to have it bang heavily atop one of the wooden countertops and not even shatter. (Those suckers were sturdy!) Talk about frustration. Nothing was going right.

(The next day, a nervous freshman with an important assignment obtained the key to the *Daily*'s one long-distance phone and dialed up the Athletic Department at Iowa, whose athletic director, we were certain, had voted for Michigan. When Bump Elliott got on the line, I could hardly speak. He was gracious with me, angry about the vote—and gave me great quotes.)

A couple of years ago the Big Ten Network aired a documentary, *Tiebreaker*, about the whole sordid chapter, and how it broke the conference out of its sniffy attitude toward bowl games not held in Pasadena. Michigan went 30–2–1 from '72 through '74 but never played a bowl game. You kids today with your 7–5 teams and your Buffalo Wild Wings Bowls, you have no idea.

Anyway. By 1976, we were beyond spoiled. We sat on the courtside press row in Philadelphia as Michigan's basketball team played for the national championship. This seemed like the natural order of things: a Final Four in March, a Rose Bowl in January. There was even a Michigan Man in the White House, Jerry Ford, former center on the football team and a Michigamua member. Old "Flip 'um Back" Ford invited current members to a reception after kicking off his '76 campaign at Crisler Arena in September. (There are three *Daily* staffers, including me, with Jerry and Betty in official White House photos of that event. School loyalty trumps politics.) Flip 'um Back of course lost to Jimmy Carter—four days before that Purdue defeat. Tough week.

Two weeks after the Purdue game Michigan hammered Ohio State, 22–0, in Columbus, to win the championship and the Rose Bowl berth. In the euphoric locker room, defensive lineman Greg Morton motioned me over. We had talked once about whether the iconic helmet was an effective recruiting tool; it had been for him, he said. Now he held out his helmet and said, "Bill, you see this? This is what I was thinking about out there. Thinking about this helmet." I totally understood. (But resisted telling him about my helmet.)

My front-page story ("BLUE ROSES!" in a huge special font) tiptoed to the edge of cheerleading but sailed through the editor-staff watchdogs. We drove home, straight through, and stopped at Maynard Street to watch the Sunday paper roar through the press downstairs.

The trip to California, three years delayed, was indeed great. Until the game. Southern Cal was just too good; a Michigan coach had told me beforehand that the NFL was eyeing as many as 15 seniors on the SC roster. Fifteen! It was true that Michigan's already weak passing game had probably atrophied over the mostly cakewalk season. Leach even allowed that he might have been more effective if he'd passed more during the season.

The *Daily* of course was shut down over the winter break. The plan was for me to write a magazine story for that first Sunday back, and I finished it promptly. It was heavy on color and outlined the now-familiar argument—Bo's one-dimensional offense sucks against good teams— which I attributed to sportswriters and pissed-off fans, because I wasn't entirely on board with it.

When I dropped the story at the *Daily* building, though, the edit-side said we needed some kind of front-page story about the game for the first edition of the semester—tomorrow's paper. It was Thursday. We couldn't wait until Sunday to acknowledge what had just happened. Bill Turque, co-editor with Rob Meachum, told me to just go get something fresh from Bo.

Right. No problem. Gulp. I wasn't even sure Schembechler was back from California. And if he was, he'd be in no mood to talk. I called Will Perry, the sports information director. He said Bo was back, but he didn't know his schedule; come down and let's see.

Which was how I ended up rehashing the Rose Bowl with a relaxed Bo in his quiet office that day. He waved me in warmly—like we were friends!—and asked me how *my* trip had been. We talked for 20 minutes or so. No rush. I brought up the outcry for a more balanced offense. "Let me tell you something," he said, leaning forward. "This is the winningest program in the country—we're not going to make any big changes."

Did complaints from the fans bother him? "I don't care about the fans." Which was true. He cared about his players, nobody else. Wouldn't Leach have been better prepared for the close game if he'd passed more? "It's absurd to think we'd abandon the most prolific offense in the country," Bo answered, going on to say of course they could improve—in all aspects of the game. And he stressed what a great team USC was.

I had what I needed. Bo walked me to his door. I did not "know" Bo, but I knew he was a nice man, friendly to any familiar face, a charmer when he wanted to be. "Next year," he said with a smile, "I'm just going to coach the first 11 games. We'll go like hell, win the championship, and then I'm going to stay home and recruit. I'll let them go to the game."

We shook hands and I left, floating with the relief that I had something to fill the column inches awaiting me. I walked back up State Street, mulling my lede. By the time I passed Pizza Bob's, I had settled on it: "Some things never change . . ."

The three-column, 42-point hed was "Defeat won't change Bo," written by an edit-sider probably hoping to convey exasperation. I read it with amusement and admiration. It was accurate. Damn straight he wouldn't change. And that was fine with me.

Was I too close to the players to see clearly? Maybe. But I was also close enough to know better than most how hard the team worked to dominate the season like that, and to come within eight points of a superior USC team, which Bo called the best in the country.

I tweaked my Sunday story accordingly, and its hed reflected that: "Did Bo's boys blow it, or did the best team win?" Sometimes I felt Bo's biggest critics were in a way the most passionate, deluded fans: They couldn't believe anyone could be better than Michigan. The coaches and players had a clearer view—and a healthier one. They took losses harder than fans, but dealt with them better.

Had I swallowed the company line? I didn't think so—I'd just presented both sides. I was finding a balance; I was learning. That's what college is about, right? I definitely understood the game better than, say, *Detroit Free Press* columnist Joe Falls, who had written that Schembechler "put an entire nation to sleep, and did indeed embarrass everyone connected with his school."

Wrong. In my Sunday story, I made sure to include a particular quote from Bo's post-game press conference: "These kids played hard and gave everything they had. You can't fault the way we tried. Southern Cal is a great, great team."

I think I got the story right.

A few months later, the NFL held its draft. When I counted up the number of players selected from each team, I blinked and felt a chill. I counted again:

USC 14, Michigan 6. The same score as the Rose Bowl. Bo wasn't kidding.

Bill Stieg worked at the *Daily* from 1973 to 1977 and was sports editor his senior year. After the 1977 Rose Bowl he covered the Wolverines for one more season, for the *Oakland Press*, where he worked for less than a year before its piggish owners forced a strike. He landed at the *Pittsburgh Post-Gazette*, where he met his wife, Jennifer Lin (thanks, piggish owners!). He worked for The Associated Press in Philadelphia and New York for 10 years, edited a magazine in Beijing, and is now articles editor at *Men's Health*. Their daughter, Cory, is a graduate of New York University, a football-free zone, and their son, Karl, graduated from film school—at the University of Southern California.

THE VA NURSES TRIAL:
MY COURTROOM EDUCATION

KEITH B. RICHBURG

Summer 1977

In the summer of 1977, what little I knew about the legal system came from my high school and college summer job working as a gofer at a downtown Detroit law firm—making endless photocopies of opinions, answering the switchboard at lunchtime, carrying the attorneys' heavy briefcases to court, and occasionally trying to deliver subpoenas using the chief lawyer's Cadillac he let me borrow.

But when I signed up to work at the summer *Michigan Daily*—kind of a rite of passage for aspiring Dailyites and future senior editors—I didn't know then that I was about to get a fast-track education in courtroom procedure, rules of evidence, cross-examination, and "jury verdict set asides," following one of the biggest, most expensive, and most unusual federal court cases in Michigan's history: the VA Hospital murder trial.

By the time it was over, some nine months later, I would become fluent talking about hospital procedures and "Code 7s," I would know all about intravenous drips, a powerful muscle relaxant known as Pavulon, and the exact number of minutes it took Pavulon to seize up the respiratory system of an unsuspecting patient.

I also learned to be skeptical, even cynical, when looking at the massive might of the federal government arrayed against an accused person with scant resources. I became jaundiced about the FBI and federal prosecutors, who were not all like the heroic and irreproachable special agent played by Efrem Zimbalist Jr. in the long-running television series. In real life, the FBI agents and prosecutors could intimidate witnesses, toy with testimony, withhold evidence from defense lawyers, and engage in tactics that—in the words of Federal District Judge Philip Pratt that stayed forever etched in my consciousness—"reduced a search for the truth to a game of five card stud poker."

That was, in short, the summer I learned how to be a reporter.

First, some quick background. I never intended that summer to become a trial reporter; I just needed the money. The *Daily*'s top editors had approached me and said they thought I might have senior editor potential, but a stint on the summer *Daily* was essential for earning your chops. And since I was one of the "Watergate babies"—lured into the excitement of journalism by following the dispatches of Woodward and Bernstein and the 1976 movie *All The President's Men*—I was eager for the chance.

The problem was, I was broke, and the *Daily* summer job didn't really pay much, just a token amount. I could ill afford to give up my pretty lucrative summer job running errands for lawyers at the Detroit firm. So I came up with an idea. The trial of two nurses accused of poisoning patients at Ann Arbor's Veterans Administration Hospital was scheduled to be held that summer. It was a big local story for the *Daily*—it was in our backyard, lots of University of Michigan med students interned there. Why don't I stay in Detroit and cover the trial, I proposed, and then I could work a few hours every week at my law firm which was just down the street from the Federal Building? Everyone agreed it was a great plan.

I actually didn't know much about the VA case even when I proposed the idea, except that it had been a huge mystery during the summer of 1975. Over six weeks, some 51 patients at the VA had suffered from breathing failures, and 10 died—some of the patients relatively healthy and in their 20s. When it was determined that something was amiss, the FBI descended on the VA with scores of agents and set up an operations room inside the facility, on Fuller Road near the University's North Campus. The federal investigation would ultimately cost some $1 million, a fortune in the 1970's, consume more than a hundred agents, and become one of the longest federal trials at that time in history.

The next summer, two intensive care unit nurses from the Philippines, Filipina Narciso and Leonora Perez, were arrested and charged with murder for allegedly injecting the victims' intravenous feeding tubes with the muscle relaxant Pavulon. The case was highly scientific. Experts hired by the bureau—scientists, toxicologists, pathologists—determined that the Pavulon, administered by syringe into an IV tube, would begin working its effects within three minutes. The case was also highly circumstantial; with no fingerprints, no murder weapon, no direct eyewitnesses, and never even a motive posited, the FBI worked backward, trying to reconstruct who was on duty during, and within minutes of, each of the mysterious breathing failures.

Besides being scientifically complex and entirely circumstantial, the case was also badly flawed, as I would soon discover.

The first problem was that many of the hospitalized victims were old and subsequently died of other causes before ever giving statements about what they saw or heard. Others who survived the poisoning episodes were ill and had only vague or faulty memories after the events. It emerged during the trial that FBI agents had resorted to a highly unusual, even bizarre technique to jog witness' memories—some 14 government witnesses were hypnotized by a New York psychiatrist, and then questioned by agents while under the hypnotically induced state. One patient, a breathing failure victim who survived and became a key government witness, only recalled when put under hypnosis seeing Leonora Perez at his bedside.

There were leads the FBI never followed up on or seemed to willfully ignore. Several witnesses told of seeing a mysterious man in a green scrub suit lurking in the hallways around the time of several poisonings—and "the man in green" would become an unknown ubiquitous presence hovering over the trial, his identity never explored, never explained. There was a VA mental patient who wandered into one victim's room around the time that victim suffered breathing difficulties and died. And, oddly, there was a nursing assistant who was granted immunity from prosecution in exchange for her testimony.

Then in March 1977, as jury selection began in the case, a bombshell hit. The *Detroit Free Press* reported that a former nursing supervisor at the Ann Arbor VA Hospital, who was being treated for mental illness and depression at a psychiatric facility, committed suicide a month earlier, after leaving behind a note exonerating the two Filipino nurses and confessing to her psychiatrist that she was the guilty party.

The nursing supervisor's suicide note and confession seemed to throw into doubt the entire prosecution case against Narciso and Perez. But there was a catch; her full psychiatric records were sealed, because of patient confidentiality, even though those records, and her talks with her psychiatrist, could make the difference between Narciso and Perez being tried or set free.

At the *Daily*, we agonized over the case, finally and reluctantly deciding on our editorial page that confidentiality trumped the rights of the Filipino nurses. "We believed that the bond of confidentiality between a doctor and his/her patient cannot be violated under any circumstances," the *Daily* wrote in an editorial. Fortunately, a week later, the deceased nurse's husband said he, too, thought the complete records should be released. On the *Daily*'s editorial page, we hailed the husband's "guts" for this courageous move, saying those records "may convince the jury there is reasonable doubt as to the guilt of Narciso and Perez." Unfortunately, the dead nurse's psychiatric records were never admitted into evidence in the court, and the jury never heard about the suicide or the confession. To me, continuing the case was a travesty.

It may be worth stopping here to ask why the FBI, with all its resources, would be intent on trying the two Filipino nurses while ignoring other potential leads. To answer that requires going back to the time, and the context, in which the murders and the trial took place.

The FBI in the mid-1970's was suffering from a series of embarrassing failures and public relations setbacks. The earlier Watergate hearings had exposed the Bureau's dark side, including warrantless bugging and surveillance of anti-war protesters and civil rights activists. In July 1975, Teamsters union leader Jimmy Hoffa disappeared from a restaurant parking lot in Bloomfield Township outside of Detroit; Hoffa was widely believed to have been kidnapped and murdered, but the FBI was never able to solve the case after frantic searching. Also that summer, California newspaper heiress Patricia Hearst was still at large, having been kidnapped by, and then later joining, the radical urban guerrilla group the Symbionese Liberation Army (she was captured in September that year).

In short, the FBI badly needed to win a big case, to restore its public reputation for competence. And the mysterious breathing attacks at the Ann Arbor VA were at the time the biggest case of all.

And there was the racial element.

Narciso and Perez were Asians, born and raised in the Philippines, at a time when anti-Asian sentiment was rife. In the spring of 1975, first Cambodia, then South Vietnam fell to the Communists, marking a humiliating defeat for the United States. There was rising concern, particularly in Detroit, over a perceived onslaught of Asian immigrants and imports. The Motor City was reeling from layoffs, blamed largely on Japanese carmakers like Toyota gaining an increasing share of the American domestic market. Filipino support groups that formed, and those who gathered outside the Federal Building with placards and "Free Narciso and Perez" T-shirts, all noted an undercurrent of anti-Asian racism that permeated the trial. One of the breathing failure victims, who had been hypnotized by the FBI, had at one point rambled on about a conspiracy of Filipino nurses in the U.S. to murder American veterans.

Ann Arbor attorney Thomas O'Brien, who represented Narciso, touched on the racial aspect at the end of the nurses' ordeal. "It may have been accidental or coincidental that the people who were charged were not American citizens," O'Brien said then, as quoted in the *Daily*. "They were not white. They were not male."

O'Brien was just 30 years old when he took the case, and he and his young partner, Michael Moran, exuded Ann Arbor cool—O'Brien with his longish, shaggy hair, Moran with his beard. I instantly took a liking to them—and not least because during breaks in the trial they would talk to me and the other reporters there regularly. These were the good guys, I thought then, the guys fighting for justice against huge odds. Not unlike the lawyers at the progressive downtown firm where I worked part time, Harry Philo and Kenneth Cockrel.

The prosecutors and the FBI agents, by contrast, seemed to me straight from central casting. They looked stern and mean, burly guys with conservative short-cropped hair. I decided if I couldn't get a job in journalism and went to law school, I definitely didn't want to be a prosecutor. (Ironically, during jury deliberations later, the lead prosecutor, Richard Yanko, told me in an exclusive *Daily* interview that he, too, didn't want to be a prosecutor and would be switching to defense work once the trial was done.)

Then there were the nurses themselves. I couldn't speak directly with them. But they appeared calm, serene . . . nice. They were petite. They smiled during the few lighthearted moments throughout the long and tedious proceedings. These two women had never even had so much as a parking ticket, and so it seemed ludicrous to me that they were now engaged in a campaign to mass murder their patients.

Day in and day out, for 10 weeks I sat through the trial, in my eyes seeing the government's case unravel. There were too many other unexplained variables, too many other possible suspects. And the prosecutors never offered a motive—by law, I learned, they weren't required to. But that lack of any motive, to me, left a gaping hole at the center of the government's case.

The *Daily*'s news and editorial sides in those days had no rigid church-state separation. When the VA murder jury went out for deliberations, we at the *Daily* ran a hard-hitting editorial, on June 30, 1977, under the headline, "Regardless of verdict, VA trial sinister farce."

"The case should never have seen the light of trial," the *Daily* wrote. "It has been a long and tiresome tale of injustice and harassment of the two nurses standing trial," the *Daily* opined. "We should all light candles for justice. . . . Justice, after all, may be dead."

So when the jury finally did reach its verdict—Narciso and Perez were found guilty of poisoning five patients—I was livid. This was a clear miscarriage of justice, I thought. It was hard to blame the jury; we reporters had seen a lot of dismissed evidence the jury never had privy to, like the dead nursing supervisor's suicide confession. But that was small consolation. Justice, as far as I thought, really was dead.

Dead, that is, until in stepped Judge Pratt. In a dramatic move, Pratt that December set aside the jury's verdict, while admonishing the prosecution for its misconduct in the case—withholding evidence from the defense, for example. Prosecutors could seek a new trial, Pratt ruled. But the jury's verdict would not stand. A federal judge setting aside a jury verdict is an extreme rarity in the criminal justice system—it simply doesn't happen often. In that case, Judge Pratt made the correct call.

I was elated. Justice had, in the end, prevailed—although the two nurses still faced a new trial. That is, until February 1978, when a new U.S. attorney, James Robinson, announced he was dropping all charges against Narciso and Perez. He cited odds the women would be acquitted, as well as "public doubt and concern as to the defendants' guilt."

"Public doubt" stuck with me. I hoped the *Daily* had played a small part in having the VA nurses set free.

I went on that summer to an internship at the *Washington Post*, which led to a full-time job at my dream paper—where I would stay for the next 34 years. For my application for that internship, I used mostly my clippings from the trial of Narciso and Perez.

I became a foreign correspondent and later foreign editor, spending 20 years at the *Post* overseas. By coincidence, or maybe serendipity, my first foreign posting in 1986 was to open a new *Washington Post* Southeast Asia bureau based in Manila. I went there with a reputation well established, as one of the reporters who covered the trial of the two nurses who were considered heroes back home.

I always wondered what happened to the two nurses. In February 2014, I found Tom O'Brien still working as a lawyer in Ann Arbor and placed a call. He told me the two women stayed in the U.S. and continued to work as nurses. Perez moved out West; Narciso remained in Southeastern Michigan and recently retired.

O'Brien remains convinced of the women's innocence, and in this case, justice was done. "The number of times when you're served up a case where you truly believe in the innocence of your client—that doesn't happen that much," he told me in a phone interview.

And in this case, he said, "The system did work."

I agree. For all my cynicism formed that summer of 1977, the system indeed did work in the end. But what happened that summer of breathing failures in the Ann Arbor VA Hospital remains a mystery that may never be solved.

Keith B. Richburg began his career at the *Michigan Daily* in 1976 as the editorial cartoonist, and later served as the *Daily*'s city hall reporter, city editor, and editorial page editor. He interned at the *Washington Post* in 1978 and 1979, and joined the *Post* full time after graduating in 1980. He stayed with the *Washington Post* for the next 33 years as a reporter on the Metro and National staffs; as a foreign correspondent for 20 years based in Manila, Nairobi, Hong Kong, Paris, and Beijing; and as the *Post*'s foreign editor from 2005 through 2007. He has since been a 2013 Fellow at the Harvard Kennedy School and a Ferris Professor of Journalism at Princeton University. He is currently a freelance writer and author splitting his time between Bangkok, Hong Kong, and New York City.

THE *DAILY* SCOOP THAT DID *NOT* SHAKE UP D.C.

RICHARD L. BERKE

November 18, 1979

For the biggest interview in my fledgling career as a Washington journalist, I wore my best jacket and tie.

I knocked on the door of a suite at the Mayflower Hotel in downtown Washington on that Saturday evening, and the most prominent person I had ever interviewed answered in his stocking feet. He was a short, 72-year-old grandfatherly-looking gentleman who seemed diminished by the high ceilinged grandeur of the stately hotel.

The man was Philip Klutznick, who one day before had been nominated as President Jimmy Carter's second Secretary of Commerce. As I made clear in the *Daily* article dated Sunday, November 18, 1979, it was Klutznick's "first private in-depth interview" since his nomination was announced. After the interview, I hustled to write the story for the next morning's *Daily*. As evidence of how excited we were about the scoop, under my byline we put in small type, "Copyright 1979. The Michigan Daily."

Copyright or not, the piece didn't set the capital ablaze. Maybe because my lede was that Klutznick said the United States must exercise its "competitive muscle in the economic struggle for markets" to control inflation. The nominee was right on message, a message that I happily scribbled into my notebook and onto the front page of the *Daily*.

So how did the *Daily* end up being part of the rollout for Klutznick, a Chicago real estate developer and prominent Democrat who was president of the World Jewish Congress? Why not start with, say, the *Wall Street*

Journal? Was Klutznick trying to win over skeptical college students who didn't think he should be the nominee? Did I doggedly hound Klutznick until he gave me his first interview?

It was then that I learned something that would guide me throughout my career: Sometimes it's just knowing the right people.

In this case, one of Klutznick's granddaughters was Amy Saltzman, my close friend and fellow editor at the *Daily*. She arranged the whole thing. (I recently asked Amy about the interview. "You seemed a little nervous," she recalled. "I told you, 'It's just my grandfather!'")

I was thrilled to get the interview. But it was not a breakthrough in American journalism—or even in my young career.

Yet the interview was an important building block as I became more and more deft at covering government and politics. First off, I learned not to put cabinet secretaries—and later the presidents I interviewed—on pedestals. They are just humans. Sometimes they pad around in socks.

The exercise of tossing questions at the nominee for Commerce Secretary gave me an early education in the world of presidential nominees, as well as my first shot at asking the questions that my colleagues and I would pose to nominees for Secretary of Commerce for years to come: Doesn't the Treasury Department hold more sway over the economy than the Commerce Department? Shouldn't the Commerce and Labor departments be combined? Weren't you picked because the president needed a political ally from your part of the country as he was gearing up to run for a second term? (In this case, Carter faced a party challenge from Senator Edward Kennedy.)

Klutznick handled all my questions nimbly and with good humor, including my query about being chosen at age 72 to be the oldest person in Carter's cabinet. "I question the judgment of those who thought they should have a man of 72 in the cabinet," he joked. (He served as Commerce Secretary for a year, until the end of the Carter presidency, and lived to age 92.)

When I look back at the yellowed *Daily* that included that story, I marvel at a University Cellar ad featuring a state-of-the-art Texas Instruments calculator for $30. It contained an "LCD display—batteries included provided 1,000 hours of continuous operation." The ad also trumpeted that the calculator had "2 memories which are retained even when calculator is turned off."

For all the advances in technology since then, journalism is still journalism. That long ago interview with Klutznick reminds me that the fundamentals of reporting that I practiced in college still hold true.

Had I had interviewed one of Obama's cabinet nominees today, I would have likely asked many of the questions I asked of Klutznick, albeit with more confidence and more wisdom—and more probing follow-ups. I no doubt would have come up with a more provocative lead.

And little did I know that the Klutznick experience would touch my life as a journalist nearly 30 years later. I was an editor at the *New York Times* when we broke the story that then New York Governor Eliot Spitzer was having a tryst with a high-priced prostitute. Where? In a suite at the Mayflower Hotel. I instantly envisioned that high-ceiled suite where I interviewed Philip Klutznick as a cub reporter. Maybe I hadn't progressed so much. Who could have imagined that I would graduate from writing a high-minded, though unremarkable, piece about the economy for the *Daily* to helping preside over the *Times'* coverage of a governor and a prostitute?

Richard L. Berke was a reporter, news editor, and managing editor at the *Michigan Daily* from 1977 to 1980. After graduating in 1980 he was a replacement reporter for the *Minneapolis Tribune*, and then went on to Columbia University's Graduate School of Journalism. After graduating from Columbia in 1981, he was hired as a reporter for the *Baltimore Evening Sun*, covering City Hall and then Washington. In 1986, he joined the *New York Times*, where he was the chief political correspondent for more than a decade and also covered the White House, Congress, and other beats. He also served as Washington editor, national editor, politics editor, assistant managing editor for news, assistant managing editor for features, and director of video content. In late 2013, he returned to Washington from New York to become the executive editor of *Politico* until late 2014. In early 2015, he took on a role with Boston Globe Media to build and become executive editor of a new national digital and print publication that will cover the booming world of life sciences. In early 2015, he took on a role with Boston Globe Media to build and become executive editor of *Stat,* a new national digital and print publication that will cover the booming world of life sciences.

REMEMBER . . . WALLY TENINGA?

ADAM SCHEFTER

November 21, 1985

Even now, nearly 30 years after the story ran in the *Michigan Daily*, it makes so little sense on so many levels.

Why would someone assign this particular piece, really any piece, to an 18-year-old freshman who never wrote for his high school newspaper and demonstrated no discernible talent that he would be able to write for his college newspaper, either.

Why would one of the sports editors agree to a "Where Are They Now?" puff-piece article, especially in a week in which Ohio State was traveling to Michigan and there were countless other compelling storylines.

Why would anyone want to read an article about a punter from the 1948 Michigan team, from a student who had no clue what it took to be a reporter, no less.

Again, nothing about it makes much sense. Yet this does: That one story represents a milestone moment in the career of that 18-year-old freshman who now reports on other more relevant football stories for ESPN.

But the story on the former Michigan punter ran Thursday, November 21, 1985, the week before Thanksgiving that year.

The headline—resting beneath the *Michigan Daily* banner—read: "Rivalry recalls unsung hero from past."

The lead was about what someone would have expected from an inexperienced, unproven, beyond-green, 18-year-old freshman—and maybe worse.

His first bylined article kicked off like this: "As The Game draws near, justice would be served to recall one of the men who helped make the Michigan-Ohio State rivalry what it is today. Remember . . . Wally Teninga?"

Remember . . . who?

It has to be one of the least imaginative, most predictable and silliest leads ever written. I mean, really. Remember . . . Wally Teninga?

Who would have remembered Wally Teninga?

He punted for Michigan in 1948, when not one student at Michigan in 1985 was even alive. Teninga went on to help implement and operate 250 Kmart stores on the West Coast, then returned to Michigan to open two wholesale Cash-and-Carry stores in the Detroit area. Teninga was a successful businessman. Yet why would students on the Michigan campus in November 1985 have remembered, or cared, about a punter from 37 years earlier?

Recently re-reading the article nearly 30 years later with a critical eye, the content was worse than the subject. Cliché after cliché. These are actual lines from the story: "Teninga most certainly was in the right place at the right time. The unheralded punter"—yet here he was being profiled 37 years later—"was called upon to try to save Michigan from defeat. Teninga would forever hold a place in the history books . . ." No rhythm, no reason, no depth, no perspective, no nothing.

This was the equivalent of an actor flubbing his lines in his first performance, a salesman botching his very first deal, a football player fumbling his first handoff in the Big House.

Of course the 18-year-old freshman had no idea of this at the time. He was too enthralled with seeing his byline for the very first time. He grabbed the first copy outside the cafeteria at the Mary Markley dorm. He looked down, saw his name in print, and could not believe it. It was, as any reporter knows and has experienced, a rush beyond words. The day his first story ran, he picked up extra copies of the *Daily* and mailed them home for his parents and family to see. He also started keeping a scrapbook of his *Michigan Daily* stories. Each one that ran would be cut out and placed in an oversized white leather-bound photo album.

How this newspaper career even started was another story, purely unintentional, completely accidental, sheer, and utter chance.

When one of Michigan's fraternity houses didn't have an open spot for another pledge . . . when Michigan's football office didn't need another student intern to pick up dirty jock straps . . . when Michigan's basketball office didn't need another student manager to pass out water bottles, the *Michigan Daily* turned away no one. It welcomed all.

So an 18-year-old freshman, from John F. Kennedy High School in Bellmore, New York, who knew nothing about sportswriting other than what he had read of it in *Newsday* and the *New York Times* at his kitchen table while growing up, showed up for work and a place to belong.

Truth is, outside of the *Michigan Daily*, nobody else showed any interest.

Then again, nobody showed much interest when he got to the *Daily*, either. The *Daily* sports bosses at that time—the sports editor being Barb McQuade, now a United States Attorney in Detroit; the associate sports editors being Dave Aretha, an author and editor in Chicago; Mark Borowsky, a senior editor and writer for ZS Associates in the Chicago area; Rick Kaplan, now the assistant managing editor at The SportsXchange; Darren Jassey, a manager for WoodWing Americas in Detroit; Adam Martin, an editor at investment firm Dimensional Fund Advisors in Austin, Texas; and Phil Nussel, the online editor of Crains' *Automotive News* in Detroit—used to conduct Sunday night meetings during which they would dole out weekly assignments to the staff of reporters. Toughest assignments went to the most qualified reporters, easiest went to the least. The 18-year-old freshman had to be the least.

During each meeting, he stood as far back in the room as possible, so that nobody would look to him and assign him a story that he feared doing. If he ever were going to accept an assignment—something he declined to do for about his first month after he walked through the door at the *Daily*—it was going to have to be for later in a week, when he had enough time to research the subject, prepare the questions, type out the story, and get it to the *Daily* bosses for their edits.

Maybe a month went by before one of the sports editors thought to assign him a piece. When they did, it was a "Where Are They Now?" piece scheduled to run that Thursday. It was no accident the article was scheduled to run on a Thursday. With homework and schoolwork piling up, the 18-year-old freshman didn't think he was capable of doing it any sooner.

So Thursday it was. Details all these years later are sketchy. Yet somehow—probably through the Michigan Athletic Department—he got a hold of Teninga's telephone number. When he reached out, Teninga didn't balk, though he had to be wondering, "Why is some cub reporter

from the school newspaper reaching out all these years later to me?"
Teninga was a gentleman, treating the student reporter with way more
respect than he deserved while crediting his team for the win over Ohio
State and the national championship they won that season.

The reporter gathered his notes, and tried to write a story the way
Newsday and *New York Times* reporters once did. It didn't work. Not
even close. The story was equally awful and meaningless. The 18-year-old
freshman deserved to be benched.

Yet for some reason, the sports editors kept letting him write. On
Wednesday, December 11, 1985, he wrote his second story, a short
harmless preview of the Penn State-Oklahoma Orange Bowl. On January
30, 1986—notice the space between assignments, speaking to the
freshman's nerves about his schoolwork and his uncertainty about his
newspaper work—there was his third story, a profile on former Michigan
offensive lineman Stefan Humphries, who had just been a part of the
Chicago Bears team that beat the New England Patriots in the Super
Bowl. Why Humphries spoke to the then 19-year-old Michigan freshman
still is baffling.

There were more and more bylines. The assignments became more
frequent. The oversized white leather-bound scrapbook filled up. A second
scrapbook, an oversized blue leather-bound photo album, eventually was
started. The subjects became more challenging. The work became more
intense. Finally, he was one of those same sports editors assigning pieces
to other young reporters the way one once had been assigned to him.

The 18-year-old freshman turned into a 22-year-old senior. During
that time, he went from reporting and writing pieces, to assigning them,
to contemplating the idea that maybe he could try to make a living in this
field. After graduation, he enrolled in graduate school at Northwestern
University's Medill School of Journalism.

Eventually, there would be newspaper stops in Seattle and Denver,
subjects ranging from Ken Griffey Jr. in Seattle to John Elway in Denver.
There would be TV stops at NFL Network in Culver City, California,
and ESPN in Bristol, Connecticut. There would be stories on the leading
men of the sport, great coaches such as Bill Belichick, Pete Carroll, and
Mike Tomlin, superstar players such as Peyton Manning, Tom Brady, and
Calvin Johnson. To this day, none of those names means any more to him
than Wally Teninga.

None ever will.

Adam Schefter was a reporter and sports editor at the *Michigan Daily* from 1985 to 1989, the year he graduated. He then attended the Medill School of Journalism in Evanston, Illinois, where he earned his master's degree in June 1990. After graduate school, Schefter interned at the *Seattle Post-Intelligencer*, now defunct, before getting a full-time job as a sports reporter in September 1990 with the *Rocky Mountain News*, also now defunct. Schefter spent 15 seasons covering the Denver Broncos for the *Rocky Mountain News* and the *Denver Post*, the longest continuous stretch any reporter has covered the team. While covering the Broncos, Schefter served as president of the Pro Football Writers of America, and also wrote books about former Super Bowl MVP Terrell Davis, former Denver head coach Mike Shanahan, and former Pro-Bowl linebacker Bill Romanowski. Schefter left the newspaper business in August 2004 to become a television reporter for the NFL Network, where he worked until 2009. In August 2009, ESPN hired Schefter to join Chris Mortensen as an NFL Insider. During his time at ESPN, Schefter has worked on multiple media platforms but rarely has reported on another punter.

"ALL'S FAIR IN LOVE AND ELECTIONS"

Relationships forged at the Daily *are built to last.*

REBECCA BLUMENSTEIN AND ALAN PAUL

Spring 1987

Our relationship began in a rather strained venue: standing side by side with several other candidates for summer editor-in-chief in a stifling hot, jam-packed room, subtly undercutting one another in one of the *Daily*'s intense elections. It wasn't an obvious setting to start a romance. And it's certainly not the image people have when they roll their eyes at the quaintness of a couple our age saying they met at the college paper.

Between us, we've interviewed powerful despots and recalcitrant rock stars; grilled disgraced CEOs and the jurors who sent them to jail; tried to crack the facade of hardened NBA players; and found ourselves stuck in inhospitable climes waiting for a source to show up. But we've never done anything quite as grueling, intimidating, or intense as run for office at the *Michigan Daily*.

The rules for the *Daily*'s fiercely democratic elections were actually quite simple: Any staff member could both run and vote. And if you wanted to have a say, you needed to stay until the end. That would be whenever the candidates and staffers exhausted themselves after hours in the Senior Office—which housed the arts and opinion staffs as well as the "long distance phone" and its log—asking and answering questions while the AP photo machine spat out images behind us. Dropping a ballot and leaving simply wasn't allowed.

No one had yet thought of putting up the campaign posters that fill the offices today; candidates could declare right up until the moment the election began, and there was no predicting what would happen. We came to this election from very different directions. One of us (Rebecca) was a favored candidate, having spent two years covering the administration beat and working as a news editor. The other (Alan) had been writing for the arts section for two years, but spent very little time hanging out or getting to know people.

REBECCA: I had decided to raise my hand for the job, which felt like a natural, if scary, step. I didn't know what to expect, as we had a very strong set of peers. I have to admit, Alan wasn't one of the competitors I was worried about. We were friendly and I thought he was a cool, unshaven arts guy, but no one knew he was running before the election. Honestly, most people didn't even seem to know who he was. He had just barely begun to make his mark as anonymous columnist Fat Al, which would become a bit of a sensation the following fall when guessing who wrote these mysterious, un-PC screeds became a campus parlor game.

ALAN: No one on staff knowing me is exactly why I ran! There had been a lot of turmoil in the arts section, with two editors who came and went in the previous few months. I had been writing a lot and getting close with the first guy, who said he wanted to groom me to replace him. Then I showed up one day, and he was gone. His replacement was forced out in a coup regarding charges of sexual harassment. I started coming around less and less, but I wanted to do more, and running for editor-in-chief seemed like a good way to be taken seriously.

REBECCA: So much of the election is a blur, but I recall making some brief remarks about ensuring that the summer paper, even though it was a weekly, was every bit as strong as the paper during the rest of the year. That was a big point of emphasis. Then we all spent hours answering questions.

ALAN: There were a few other people running, including a small crew who everyone knew were the real candidates; Becky was clearly, deservedly, in that group. I was actually even a darker horse than the late Henry Park, the Maoist editor of the opinion page, because he had his cadre. I was proud when Henry told me he had voted for me; he may have been the only one.

We both achieved our real goals in that election: Rebecca was voted editor and Alan became better known to the staff, a precursor to growing much more active over the next year. The election was also the beginning of our real relationship, a friendship that deepened while working together on the skeleton *Daily* summer staff.

Over the summer, we teamed up to become the *Weekend* magazine co-editors for the coming year. Fellow staffers began to think there was something going on with us, especially when we appeared arms around each other on the cover of *Weekend* magazine as part of an inane fashion issue the business staff foisted upon us. We were actually still setting one another up with housemates and friends and wouldn't become a couple until a month before graduation, and by then we understood each other very well, having experienced the *Daily* soap opera together.

The intensity of *Daily* debates was magnificent. As a peer-led paper, we all taught each other how to write and report. We edited each other's stories, and then tore them to bits on the Crit Board. We worked ridiculously late into the night writing stories, never quite able to get ahead of the crush of deadlines and school work.

We also disagreed about how to handle stories or crises or whatever issues pulsated through campus, such as when the University became one of the first in the country to try to regulate hate speech, neatly dividing the staff between those worried about the imposition of a much-feared code of conduct and those wanting to do something about a worrisome spate of racial incidents. We attempted to navigate the parameters of political correctness before most of us had even heard the term.

We helped each other on bad nights when one of us missed deadline and incurred the wrath of the incomparable Lucius Doyle, the printing production manager who laid out the pages with an X-Acto knife that he often wielded like a weapon, seeking to intimidate. Any word change meant a trip back downstairs to explain its importance to Lucius, who would stare a hole through you if he thought your rationale was lame. (Lucius' approval of us as a couple was one of our earliest signs that our relationship might just have legs, and a summer evening spent drinking vodka and Squirt on his patio is an indelible memory.)

An atmosphere like this leads to intense relationships. The staff went through many upheavals, none any more heated than the attempt to eradicate the suffix "man" through an inclusive language policy. The sports staff seemed OK with "first-year student" instead of "freshman," except when modified by "redshirt," but drew the line in front of "first base person." This attempted change in *Daily* policy led to staff meetings and votes that made the elections seem like child's play.

These types of debates were equally likely to make you laugh or cry, and if you found someone who laughed when you laughed and cried when you cried, you might just be onto something. At least two other enduring relationships started during our time at the *Daily* (Jeff Rush and Martha Sevetson and Steve Knopper and Melissa Ramsdell. Both couples worked at various journalism jobs; Knopper remains a contributing editor at *Rolling Stone*). We can't speak for them or anyone else who's had a long marriage that began at 420 Maynard, but we believe that a relationship that emerges intact from such a heated environment is forged in molten lava and ready to be road tested.

If you can survive "first base person" and accusations of being a racist; running for office against each other; and attempted Marxist coups, then the rest of life's travails are a breeze. And there's nothing quaint about that.

Rebecca "Becky" Blumenstein worked at the *Daily* from 1985 to 1989 as a reporter, news editor, *Weekend* editor, and editor-in-chief. She is the deputy editor-in-chief of the *Wall Street Journal*, where she started covering General Motors in the Detroit bureau in 1995. She has held a wide range of jobs there, including China bureau chief, foreign editor, and page one editor.

Alan Paul was a *Daily* writer, arts editor, *Weekend* editor, and columnist (under the nom de plume Fat Al) from 1985 to 1988. He is a senior writer for *Guitar World* and *Slam* magazines and a former award-winning columnist for wsj.com. He has written for the *New Yorker*, *Wall Street Journal*, *People,* and many other publications and websites. He is also the author of *Big in China* and the bestseller *One Way Out: The Inside History of the Allman Brothers Band.*

They were married at the Michigan League in 1993 and have three children.

FROM CRITIC TO NEWS REPORTER

BETH FERTIG

September 11, 1987

In the summer of 1987, I began my gradual transformation from *Michigan Daily* music critic to news reporter, all because of an encounter with Jello Biafra.

Biafra was the lead singer for the Dead Kennedys, a San Francisco punk rock band that had gotten into legal trouble for its album artwork. The band was prosecuted for allegedly distributing hardcore pornography to minors. While interning at *SPIN*, I was lucky enough to attend a seminar Biafra gave in New York City that summer, and that experience changed me when I returned to Ann Arbor.

I had started writing for the *Daily* as a freshman in the fall of 1984. Like all the other wannabe staff writers, I had to work a few evenings in the news department learning how to copy edit AP stories ripped straight off the wire. But I was more interested in music. I'd grown up in Long Island, New York loving the new bands featured on WLIR Radio and reading *Rolling Stone* religiously. Gradually, I migrated over to the arts department and asked to review some albums.

I didn't have the encyclopedic knowledge of the diehard music fans I met that year in East Quad and at WCBN-FM, the University's student-run radio station. I couldn't even write all that well about music—I was always running out of adjectives. I also certainly didn't have enough attitude to be a legit rock critic. And I was a girl in what was definitely a boy's world.

But I wore lots of black, wrote proficiently enough, and turned in my copy on time. Even better, I made sure other critics on staff turned in their copy by deadline—even if that meant buying them bags of Hawaiian Kettle potato chips (ahem, Mike Rubin). This was a big deal when Lucius Doyle ran the layout room with his X-Acto blade, yelling at students, "Where's my copy?!"

By 1987 I was the *Daily*'s music editor, and it seemed like a natural move to try an internship at *SPIN*. My parents were living in Manhattan, so I had a place to stay. The annual New Music Seminar was taking place in New York City that summer, too, which would be a good opportunity for me to make some connections and come up with story ideas for my return to the *Daily*.

This big junket was in a Times Square hotel, and one of the seminars featured Jello Biafra of the Dead Kennedys. I knew about the band's legal problems, so I was intrigued to see what he'd say. The band was being prosecuted over its album "Frankenchrist," which featured a poster with phallic imagery by the artist H.R. Giger. This incident became a rallying cry for those who wanted to protect artistic free expression, and for those who wanted to crack down on material they deemed inappropriate for minors. Tipper Gore led that movement, with her Parents Music Resource Center.

I went to Biafra's talk and was blown away by his eloquence and passion. At one point, in a very Khrushchev-ian move, he took off a shoe and passed it around the audience seeking donations of money. He was broke, and he couldn't afford his defense team. People cheered for him— not as a rock star but as a cause. If this could happen to him, it could happen to any musician who struck a wrong note, so to speak.

When I returned to school a few weeks later, I was determined to write about the trial in some way. It was happening far away in California, but I stayed on top of the news by reading other newspapers (a little bit of a challenge pre-Internet). The case ended with a hung jury, and that's when I decided it was time for me to write an article.

By then I was much less interested in music, and more intrigued by its societal implications. Seeing Biafra shake that shoe, and watching the debate over censorship awakened something in me. When I wrote the article for the *Daily*, I felt a lot more confident than I ever felt as a critic trying to describe music.

Don't get me wrong. I loved my time at the *Daily* writing about music— even if I suspected all along that it wasn't really my thing. Through my job at the *Daily*, I spent an evening talking to Henry Rollins about his poetry after a Black Flag show at the Nectarine Ballroom on campus. (Best part: He told me he had been offered the role of Jim Morrison in a movie about the Doors, but didn't want to be remembered as "the guy who played Jim.") I got to see amazing blues, rock, and international artists play in Ann Arbor and Detroit for free. But increasingly, I wanted to write about what was happening in the world around me.

Today, when I read my article about the Biafra trial I'm impressed by how much ground I covered explaining the case. It still reads pretty well—though it's a little dense, and my sentences feel very long (I couldn't do that in radio).

I am surprised to see that I editorialized a little. I wrote about how the hung jury represented the stupidity of the entire legal case—I guess I couldn't be totally neutral. But I'm proud of this story and glad I put a little of my own outrage in the piece. After all, I was still only 21. I had plenty of time to learn how to be a better reporter. The *Daily* gave me my start.

Beth Fertig was a writer, music editor, and arts editor at the *Michigan Daily* from 1984 to 1988. After graduation she worked as a local reporter for two years at the Tab chain of newsweeklies in the Boston metro area. Fertig had a temporary brush with academia, earning a master's degree in social sciences at the University of Chicago in 1991. But she returned to journalism by volunteering for a public radio program in Boston. After a couple years of freelancing she was hired by WNYC in New York, the nation's largest public radio station, in 1995. She covered the administration of former Mayor Rudolph Giuliani, the September 11 terrorist attacks, city infrastructure, and former mayor Michael Bloomberg's public school reforms. She took off in 2008 to write a book about education called *Why Cant U Teach Me 2 Read?* Beth's current title is Contributing Editor for Education at WNYC. Her reports are frequently heard on National Public Radio. She won the prestigious Alfred I. DuPont–Columbia University Award for broadcast news reporting in 2001 and has won many other local and national awards, including an Edward R. Murrow Award.

UNRAVELING AN INTERNET FANTASY

JOSH WHITE

January to March 1995

Journalists had mobbed the front steps of the U.S. District Court in Detroit, and I timidly blended in, craning my neck to catch a glimpse of the defendant and his lawyer making their way outside. I briefly lost my footing when a photographer elbowed me aside, and I wondered for a second if I really belonged there, an 18-year-old freshman at the center of one of the biggest Internet criminal cases yet to arise anywhere in the world.

Douglas Mullkoff, an attorney representing a University of Michigan sophomore who had been arrested for posting a series of graphic rape and torture stories online, stepped forward. Professional reporters from the Detroit papers and television stations began shouting. Mullkoff stopped, scanned the crowd, and pointed in my direction: "Josh White, the *Michigan Daily*, do you have a question?"

I don't remember what question I posed, I wish I could. But that was the moment when I knew I was going to be a journalist for the rest of my life. The work we as students had done at the *Daily* played a role in what was happening that afternoon, our reporting and explaining of a complex situation had rooted out facts no one else had uncovered—helped people think differently—and lives had changed as a result. It felt like all that we were doing really *mattered*.

The situation began in January 1995, when a University alum in Moscow found a gruesome tale of kidnapping, rape, torture, and murder on an online bulletin board called "alt.sex.stories." The posting appeared to include the name of a real University of Michigan student as the victim, and many of the details could have related to a realistic attack—or plan for an attack—on that student. The concerned alum abroad then notified the University.

Within a day, authorities were interviewing Michigan sophomore Jake Baker and searching his dorm room and computer accounts. There they found alarming stories and email conversations Baker had written, evidence, they said, that Baker was dangerous. University President James Duderstadt suspended him a little more than a week later, and then in early February, the FBI arrested Baker and he was denied bail, considered a serious threat to harm others.

Though not that long ago, public use of the Internet was still in its infancy in early 1995, and it was a mystery to most people. As a freshman arriving in Ann Arbor that fall I had received my first email address— the coveted @umich.edu domain—and soon after began conversing with friends using telnet. The Internet as we know it now didn't really exist yet; none of my friends had cellphones, and the best way to reach a *Daily* editor was by calling a pager. Several *Daily* reporters and editors were starting to play games against each other remotely and would taunt each other by sending messages to the networked printers in the newsroom and throughout campus.

When a University student was suspended and arrested for posting stories to the Internet, it was of wide curiosity and appeared to be one of the government's first attempts to deal with crimes of violence in cyberspace. It also had all sorts of First Amendment implications. Were these stories, posted in relatively plain view for the world to see, something that could be considered threats? Was Baker potentially dangerous based on his writings? Could federal authorities regulate such speech on the Web?

I got involved in the story as a fledgling crime reporter after the initial reports about Baker's suspension came out, having the honor of working with future editor-in-chief Ronnie Glassberg and then-editor-in-chief Michael Rosenberg—both of whom have pursued careers in journalism. The *Daily* at the time was full of aspiring journalists who cared deeply about what we were doing, and the conversations about the case were filled with thoughtful analysis and an understanding that we were uniquely suited to present the information to the University community.

Within days of the arrest, I learned that Baker's roommate was in one of my classes, and I began to try to understand who this guy was. From the government's perspective, he was a predator who needed to be locked behind bars. His friends characterized Baker as a diminutive, bookish student who many were surprised was capable of writing the things his stories contained. But what the stories contained was by almost any measure pretty awful.

We worked tirelessly to get to every angle. Though the student named in the story did not want to talk to us—and we never identified her publicly—Rosenberg established a dialogue with her family, and we were able to explain to readers how it might feel to have your name associated with such a thing. We talked to students, to civil liberties experts, to law enforcement officials. And I established a dialogue with Baker's mother, a creative writing teacher in Ohio.

Our breakthrough came on February 10, 1995, during a detention hearing for Baker in federal court. Prosecutors argued that Baker was a danger to society, and some professional journalists in the room leafed through "Internet for Dummies" books to catch the Web terms as they arose. Some amount of fluency with the University's computer systems proved invaluable, because we were operating on the same systems Baker was. When documents containing Baker's email conversations about rape were entered into evidence, I noticed that there was header information on one of the emails, indicating that Baker had corresponded with a man in Virginia.

So I emailed the man in Virginia.

It turned out that on January 13, 1995, before the University or the FBI became aware of Baker's stories, Baker had corresponded with this man about his motivations, a snapshot in time before Baker knew anyone would view his stories as potentially dangerous. The man had come across Baker's work online and emailed him directly to convey his concerns about the nature of the stories and also forwarded his concerns to the University. Baker responded, according to emails I discovered.

"My stories are harmless diversions. I have never hurt anybody, and never plan on hurting anybody," Baker wrote to the man. ". . . I have remained honest to you people, simply to express the fact that I would never do the things in my stories."

Baker went on to say that he posted the stories with his real name because he invited scrutiny of what he characterized as fiction, and he said those advocating for him to pull them down were akin to censors. In an email, the man told me: "I was merely concerned about a person who would pass off as 'erotica' a story about rape, mutilation and snuff."

We printed that story in mid-February, and Baker's lawyers used the material to bolster their argument that Baker was simply writing fiction and that his fiction was protected speech. After a psychological examination determined that Baker wouldn't act out the fantasies he penned, Baker was released on bond in March.

When Mullkoff's courthouse news conference ended, he grabbed me and said to meet him around the side of the courthouse a few minutes later. There, he had arranged for Baker to give his only interview about the case. He talked with me about what it was like to be a student and to be held in a federal prison. He talked about what it was like to celebrate his 21st birthday behind bars. He talked, I listened, the *Daily* printed it.

The lessons of that case have driven much of my approach to journalism since: The importance of listening to all sides and trying to understand their perspectives, digging into every detail because you don't know which one is going to yield the most important information, and bringing readers information they can't get anywhere else. It was then that I realized journalism is truly a public service, an opportunity to explain and give context, and get people to think about the world around them.

But while that moment was the inspiration, it was the rest of my *Daily* experience that solidified my commitment to the profession. Working with enormously talented people who were doing it for the love of it gave me that same ethos. I have, every day since, aimed to emulate that passion and will always be thankful for the guidance, patience, and dedication of everyone I worked with at 420 Maynard.

Josh White was a *Michigan Daily* news reporter and editor from 1994 to 1996 and editor-in-chief in 1997. After graduating in 1998, White took a summer internship at the *Washington Post* and hasn't left. From 1998 to 2004 he was a crime and courts reporter in Virginia and covered the Washington area sniper case. From 2004 to 2008 he was a military correspondent, covering the Pentagon and twice embedding with U.S. troops in Iraq. After working as an investigative reporter focusing on law enforcement and sex crimes, White became the *Post*'s education editor in 2012.

MY BIG HOUSE

JOSHUA RICH

September 20, 1995

It was the best time I ever had in the big house. On a brisk Ann Arbor morning in the fall of 1995, I left my dorm room, put on my jacket, and walked the long way across campus to work on an assignment for the *Michigan Daily*. I was giddy to see what would unfold after I entered the arena and wound my way into the sea of seats. But I was not a sports writer, and my big house was not *The* Big House.

Nope, I was a movie critic, one of the fortunate few who had been tapped to weigh in on films for the *Daily*. I loved the job, almost as much as I loved the movies themselves. That's right: I was the kid in the freshman dorm whose walls were plastered with movie posters and bookcase was filled with a large library . . . of videotapes. No doubt about it, I was hooked. And thanks to the *Daily*, I got my fix on a weekly basis.

I watched everything. Some evenings, I would walk from Alice Lloyd Residence Hall to the Michigan Union, where I would pick up the city bus to Briarwood Mall, so that I could hang out in the old United Artists multiplex and catch the latest fare. (Remember *Terminal Velocity*, the Charlie Sheen skydiving spy thriller? Neither do I. But my clip file says that I gave it a C- grade.) Other times, I would borrow a friend's car and drive way out to the Showcase Cinemas on Carpenter Road. There, I would luxuriate in the cushy seats that squeaked a little bit when I leaned back while watching an action flick like legendary director Ridley Scott's *G.I. Jane*. (You know, the one for which a buffed-up Demi Moore won her second consecutive Golden Raspberry Award for Worst Actress.) Or, all too often, I would just stay in town, ditch class, and pop over to the State Theatre to catch an afternoon showing of *Pulp Fiction* for the fourth time. (Or was it the 14th?)

Fun as all that was, however, nothing compared to that one morning I spent in the big house. Sure, there was The Big House, Michigan Stadium, where I rooted for the football team as it won a national championship during my senior year. But my big house was another great Ann Arbor amphitheater filled with history and brimming with gilded charm. The great film critic Pauline Kael once wrote a book called "I Lost it at the Movies." Well, I lost it at the Michigan Theater.

During the four years I spent at Michigan and the *Daily*, the Michigan Theater was my real home. It was where I sat with hundreds other folks to revel in a re-release of *2001: A Space Odyssey*, or to listen to the warbles of the Barton Organ accompanying some silent classic, or to see a few of the great features in the Ann Arbor Film Festival, or to catch a live touring show like Penn & Teller's magic and comedy act. To me, the big house at 603 East Liberty Street was my house.

And then on that morning in 1995, it was actually all mine.

My assignment was to review an obscure Chinese drama called *The Story of Xinghua*. Now, movies themselves can often be very dramatic, but the fundamental act of reviewing a movie does not normally lend itself to high drama or a compelling narrative. There are no touchdowns. No tear gas. No visiting dignitaries to wow a crowd. Instead, basically, you've got a dark theater, a brightly lit screen, a few other people in the audience—and you. That's it. Watch the movie. Go home.

This morning was different. I showed up at the 9 a.m. show time, reporter's notebook and pencil in hand. But nobody was there. Box office? Empty. Front doors? Locked. Marquee? Dark. I waited. Was I in the right place? At the right time? Was I supposed to go to the Ann Arbor 1 & 2 or the Fox Village theater instead? I grew concerned. (And, of course, it being the 20th century, I didn't have an iPhone in my pocket.)

I knocked on the door. After a few moments, a rumpled guy with bleary eyes walked slowly out of the shadows from inside the lobby and cracked open the front door.

"Are you Josh?" he asked me.

"I am. From the *Michigan Daily*?" I said, just trying to make sure.

"Yep. Right. Good," he said. "I'm the projectionist. Come on in."

He motioned me forward and I stepped inside a place that I had visited dozens of times before, though never like this. We walked through the entryway, past the dormant popcorn machine, and dusky concession stand, and into the grand space where the sparkling staircase leads to the balcony and the polished wood doors swing open to the orchestra.

We stopped.

"When does the movie start?" I asked.

"Whenever you're ready," the guy said, smiling. "You're the only one here. Sit wherever you'd like, and I'll start when you're all set."

Wow. It hit me—I had the whole place to myself! This magnificent building, this restored motion picture palace filled with 1,700 seats and the memories of millions of moviegoers over more than 67 years, was all mine for the morning. Amazing.

But I had no time to relish my good fortune because I had yet to enter the auditorium and pick my seat. Balcony or orchestra? Front or back? It was still in the days before movie theaters offered reserved seating, but on that morning every last seat was reserved for me. Ummm . . . orchestra!

I tugged on the heavy doors and walked quickly along the aisle, finding a row halfway down and a seat halfway across. Right in the middle. The polished organ gleamed up to the left of the stage. The seats spread out from me on all sides. I looked up to the balcony but saw and heard nothing other than the projectionist setting up his booth.

I took off my jacket and sat down in my seat. Notebook out. Pencil at the ready. Eyes focused and mind spinning with delight for my great luck and in anticipation of the film that was about to unspool, I watched as the soft glow on the faux windows high above the orchestra faded out and the lights went down. The ruby red curtain parted and the silver screen behind it lit up. The show—my show—was about to begin.

Joshua Rich was a movie critic, columnist, and arts editor at the *Michigan Daily* from 1994 to 1998. A week after graduation, he started working at *Entertainment Weekly* magazine, which hired him based in part on his *Daily* review of *G.I. Jane*. Seven years later, he found himself interviewing Ridley Scott, face to face in the director's L.A. office, about Scott's latest movie and trying not to reveal that he had panned *G.I. Jane* by writing that it was "like a sadomasochistic Madonna video set in Vietnam." (In other words, it was no *Story of Xinghua*.) He is now a lawyer living in Los Angeles, having worked as a writer and editor for 11 years at *Entertainment Weekly*, a reporter for *U.S. News & World Report*, and the editor-in-chief of the *Loyola of Los Angeles Law Review*.

DUDE, I'M GOING TO FINISH MY PIZZA

MICHAEL ROSENBERG

September 28, 1995

On the afternoon of my 21st birthday, the pager on my hip buzzed, which seemed futuristic at the time but now makes me feel 132 years old. I was eating with friends at Pizzeria Uno on South University and celebrating the fact I had not died of alcohol poisoning the night before. It had been close.

After a few buzzes, I went to a pay phone and called the number on the pager. A news editor at the *Michigan Daily* answered and told me that University President James J. Duderstadt had resigned. I was the *Daily's* editor-in-chief.

"It's a big story," he said.

(Really? So we shouldn't bury it on page 7? Thanks!)

When news breaks, the best journalists react immediately. I, on the other hand, finished my pizza. This was before anybody had to rush a story onto the Internet. I knew it would be a long day (they were all long days) and this was my last chance to think clearly, and possibly to eat. When we were done eating, I went off to 420 Maynard.

It would be years before I heard the phrase "flooding the zone" to describe a news outlet covering every aspect of a story with a slew of reporters. But I already knew what it meant, and I knew it was time to do it.

We struggled every day at the *Daily* with the balance between what our readers cared about (parking tickets, the crossword puzzle) and matters of slightly more importance (there are people starving in Africa, and you ungrateful bastards are worried about parking tickets?). This conflict was especially apparent in editorial board meetings. There were always writers who earnestly believed that peace in the Middle East was just one well-written editorial away.

There was no conflict when the president of the school resigned. This was a story we could own. It affected every segment of the University, and every one of our readers. No other publication could say that. We convinced the business staff to give us extra pages. We assigned people to write about Duderstadt's choice, his legacy, the effect on various departments, highlights and lowlights, possible successors. We were all energized—both by the feeling of covering a big story and, I think, by the knowledge that we would cover it more thoroughly than anybody else.

That afternoon, I did a radio interview with a host who mistook me for both an expert and somebody who knew how to do a radio interview. I distinctly remember saying that Duderstadt was "neither the best nor the worst president the University ever had," and as I bathed in the cologne of my own objectivity, I was only vaguely aware that what I said was meaningless. I might as well have said Duderstadt had not ended poverty in America or murdered 1,000 people. A journalist does not need *that much* middle ground.

By the time we met deadline that night (ha!), we had produced more than 20 stories about Duderstadt's resignation, along with a picture of The Dude on the phone in his office, with the headline "CALLING IT QUITS."

The reaction on campus was surely more muted than I remember. But I know some students were impressed by our coverage.

I had come to the *Daily* to write, stayed because I loved it, and got elected editor-in-chief because I had spent more time in the building than anybody else.

Nobody can prepare you for leading a staff of your peers in an enterprise you are just learning yourself. I don't know if our coverage was great that day, but we had at least *tried* to be great, and tried in the right ways. I had the significant feeling that night that maybe we did know what the hell we were doing.

That is the beauty of the *Daily* to me. Some other college newspapers have full-time faculty advisors, university funding, or academic departments that funnel students to them. The *Daily* had none of that. We had to figure it out ourselves every day. Sometimes the process was sloppy, and sometimes the product was sloppy. But the product was ours, and most days, we could be proud of it.

I firmly believe the freedom at the *Daily* spurred our creativity more than any formal curriculum would have. I've been a professional journalist for almost 20 years, and I've met a lot of people who were churned out by J-school machines.

Their journalism educations were probably smoother. I still believe ours was better.

For four years, people teased me about spending so much time at the *Daily*, but the hours only increased every year. As editor-in-chief, I worked so late that once in a while I would come home to my apartment and find the next day's *Detroit Free Press* and *Detroit News* outside my door. Sometimes I slept on the couch in the photo department. I'm sure I did not have to spend as much time at the *Daily* as I did, but I learned one of the most valuable lessons in life, and it's not a journalism lesson: If you love what you do, it won't feel like work, and you will never feel overworked. It helps if you love the people who do it alongside you.

When Duderstadt spoke at our commencement that spring, he mentioned that students had excelled in so many places on campus.

"Even the *Michigan Daily*," he said.

Thousands cheered. Well, a few of us did.

Michael Rosenberg worked at the *Michigan Daily* from 1992 to 1996 and served as editor-in-chief as a senior. He was a longtime columnist at the *Detroit Free Press* before becoming a senior writer at *Sports Illustrated*. He has also worked at the *Sacramento Bee*, *Philadelphia Inquirer*, *Chicago Tribune*, and *Washington Post*. He is the author of *War As They Knew It: Woody Hayes, Bo Schembechler, and America in a Time of Unrest*. He lives in Ann Arbor with his wife Erin (*Daily* Class of 1998) and three children.

FOOTBALL PLAYER BY DAY, PHOTOGRAPHER BY NIGHT

DHANI JONES

1997–2000

It was one of those moments in class when you're daydreaming. Sitting there, when the professor had officially lost me, I decided then and there that a new project was to be had. Sure, the University of Michigan football team took up most of my afternoon, and pre-med studies the rest, but I had time. I swore up and down that because photography was my passion, I would make it fit in my schedule no matter what. And so when that fateful class ended, I took off running to the *Michigan Daily* and submitted my application to join the photo staff.

I'd like to think I remember the newsroom like it was yesterday, but since graduating 15 years ago, the memories are fading. What I do remember is the hustle and bustle of students, who had clearly worked on their high school newspaper staffs, yelling back and forth about getting the next issue out. I was green but ready to be seasoned and take a hold of a brand new camera. There were so many options I could choose from, and the expensive lenses were my calling. With a press pass, I could be a sideline "photog" at the games my fellow student-athletes were playing.

And so that's what I did—during all my spare time. I cruised up and down State Street, from the *Daily* to sporting events, being the consummate curious individual my Montessori education taught me to be. Wearing an orange coat, with my backpack strapped to my body, and a 400mm lens camera hanging off the side, I walked into Crisler Arena and used my press pass and equipment to get in front of all the action. Covering hundreds of basketball games, gymnastics meets, and other sporting events was a sublime experience peppered with the occasional fan wondering if the guy with the camera was actually me. Sometimes I'd respond by saying, "yes," it was me, only for the inquisitor to pose a frown and respond, "Yeah right." Why in the world would a Michigan football player want to shoot photography during his "spare time?" Wasn't there practice or study hall?

You see, my adventure at the University of Michigan had many interesting twists and turns, and I always look back and wonder, how did I make it out of the maize of blue? My mother and father, being Michigan graduates, set a precedent but oftentimes as a trailblazer you have to live by your own credo. "Carpe diem" was my motto in everything I chose to do. And when I decided to illustrate my experience in a photographic manner, I made sure to capture moments students would remember for the rest of their lives.

So from East Quad to the Big House, I can say it was a creative experience that let me follow my passion and helped set the stage for my career today.

Dhani Jones lived a dual college life as a Michigan football player and *Michigan Daily* photographer from 1997 to 2000. He was then drafted to the New York Giants and later played for the Philadelphia Eagles and Cincinnati Bengals. During his 11-year dominance on the football field as a linebacker, Jones launched his first creative agency, VMG Creative, filmed his hit series on the Travel Channel, *Dhani Tackles the Globe*, and authored *The Sportsman* (2011). Following his NFL retirement in 2012, Jones teamed up with Spike TV to host shows *PlayBook 360* and *GT Academy*, was featured in GQ and ESPN magazine, and produced his own show, *In the Zone with Dhani Jones*. In 2013, Jones launched his second creative agency, Proclamation, and a private equity company, Qey Capital, in Cincinnati, Ohio, the last city he played in the NFL and his current home base. Photography is still one of his passions today.

DATELINE BEIJING

MARGARET MYERS

February 19, 1997

I have one of those adventurous moms who calls you in the middle of a semester at college to ask if you'll go to China with her. In 1997, I took her up on just such an offer. It was February of my sophomore year, and I was a *Michigan Daily* photographer when I flew to Beijing with my family for a week. I missed class—and subsequently had to drop my arduous chemistry course—but it was worth it. Because, in a lot of ways, I got my diploma from the College of the *Michigan Daily*, and this trip was a prescient moment for my future career.

We happened to be in Beijing when former Chinese leader Deng Xiaoping died. This is the man who succeeded Mao Zedong and opened the door for China to move into the modern global economy. Kind of a big story, right? I thought so.

The next morning I was eager to witness how people were grieving. The city was actually very subdued, but I happened to capture a photo of an old man dressed in his proletarian blue "Mao suit" and cap. He was sitting on a little stool just off the side of the street and reading a newspaper—a state-run one I assumed—with a large photo of Deng on the cover.

It was nothing spectacular, but I thought, wouldn't it be neat if I could get this newsworthy nugget to the *Daily*?

Now the fun part: How to get it there.

I call the newsroom in Ann Arbor from a payphone in the lobby of our hotel. The dayside editor Will Weissert answers. "It's Marge. So I'm in China . . ." I tell him and explain the details. He says he'd love a photo.

Photo by Margaret Myers.

I pick up a Chinese phone book and find the number for the AP office in Beijing. They tell me they're a little busy, but to come by after dinner. So my dad and I hopped in a taxi that night and made our way to their office, a cramped apartment in a large residential-looking concrete compound.

Remember, this is 1997, so I shot film. The guys processed my negatives—it's a 15-minute procedure involving a can opener and a chemical called blix—and scanned my photo into their machine that would blow my image across the wire. The best part was waiting for my negatives because I got to hang with the guys and pretend I was a real journalist. They treated me like one, too, which was the coolest feeling in the world to a 20-year-old cub.

At this point, the modern me would have just shot a text over to Will in the newsroom saying, "It's in. Let me know if you have questions." Of course, I didn't do that. But wouldn't you know it, the *Daily* picked up my photo, and the next morning it was smack-dab in the center of A1.

Almost 20 years later, this is still my dad's favorite story to tell at family gatherings. If it wasn't for him, I might have forgotten about the experience. I mean, who cares, I was just a kid then, so it doesn't count. We were kid journalists running a kid paper. But of course we weren't, and it wasn't.

My training at the *Daily* got me to where I am today. It got me my first job shooting for a newspaper in Manassas, Virginia. It gave me the confidence to try my hand at being a journalist in Latin America where I worked in Guatemala and Mexico for five years. It was the four years of covering one of the greatest college sports program in America (Go Blue!) that got me in the door at ESPN.

I'm proud of my University of Michigan diploma, but I got my real education from the *Michigan Daily*.

Margaret Myers joined the *Michigan Daily* as a photographer in 1996 and served as photo editor from 1998 to 1999. After graduating from Michigan, she moved to Washington, D.C., and worked as a staff shooter for the *Daily Journal*, a newspaper that covered Virginia's Prince William County. With no Spanish training, she moved to Guatemala City in 2000 and joined a small group of journalists who launched the *Guatemala Post*. She was the original copy editor, designer, and photographer. After a year she took an opportunity to go north to Mexico City, where she served as the assistant features editor for the *News*, a 50-year-old

English-language daily. Sadly, it folded in 2002. For the next several years she freelanced for newspapers in the United States, including the *Dallas Morning News* and the *Detroit Free Press*. In 2007, she moved to Texas *y'all* to become the features editor at the *Amarillo Globe-News*. In 2010 she became an editor for ESPN's high school sports site. Sadly, that also folded. But that's OK, because she now works for her other favorite network, PBS, where she is the digital news editor for *PBS NewsHour*.

BIG MAN, BIG IMPACT

MARK SNYDER

March 8, 1998

The foot arrived like an asteroid, prepared to end my own personal Earth.

Only 21 years old, I still had much to live for, but Robert Traylor was about to render me extinct.

It was March 8, 1998, and monstrous Michigan basketball player Robert Traylor nearly buried me.

Listed at 6-foot-8, 300 pounds, but surely carrying a few more pounds than advertised, the massive man had just carried his Michigan basketball team to the inaugural Big Ten Tournament title at Chicago's United Center, and he was looking to celebrate.

Instead of the modern circumstance where a small stage is erected at mid-court and the players wait patiently to be honored, Traylor decided he was going to the stands the quickest way possible—over the press table, no matter who was in the way.

He planted one of those size 18s on the courtside counter and launched himself over two press row tables and a permanent railing, showing remarkable grace as he avoided landing on me and ending my career before it began.

From my perspective, a moment of pure terror, fighting off the unexpected. From his, pure exaltation.

He just wanted to share it with his family, including his grandmother, Jessie Mae Carter, who helped raise him in Detroit with apparently little money, but he had basketball as his escape. So their embrace held much more than just the momentary victory.

"I didn't have a chance to say much," Traylor said that day, written in the next day's *Daily*. "She did all the talking."

Scoring 17.3 points and grabbing 12.7 rebounds in the three-game burst, Traylor's MVP moment reminded everyone what he could do when motivated. The previous spring, he had earned the same award, carrying the Wolverines to the NIT championship, and later starred during the December 1997 tournament in Puerto Rico.

This Big Ten Tournament title capped a season of turmoil, which started the previous summer when the Ed Martin booster scandal began to emerge, leading to coach Steve Fisher's firing. The job was handed to freshly arrived assistant Brian Ellerbe as a season-long interim coach, and he guided the Wolverines to a fourth-place Big Ten finish.

Everyone knew that team had elite talent, with Traylor and guard Louis Bullock leading the way, but only played to their potential when inspired, leading to one of the all-time roller coaster seasons.

They lost the season opener at home to Western Michigan, then squeaked by Detroit by only a point. They lost at lowly Bradley, then the next game upset No. 1 Duke at Crisler Arena, just the second top-ranked win in program history.

They would beat No. 19 Syracuse by 32 in Puerto Rico, yet later lose by 28 to unranked Indiana. Seven weeks later, they put a historic whipping on those same Hoosiers at Crisler, winning by 48.

There was no predicting Traylor or that group all season so the tournament title just fit. As did their sudden NCAA Tournament flameout in the second round in Atlanta, losing to a UCLA team that lost its best player, guard Baron Davis, in the middle of the game to injury.

A fitting end to Traylor's Michigan career as he would declare for the NBA draft just over a week later.

Three bizarre years started with immense expectations, as Traylor arrived from Detroit Murray-Wright High School as Michigan's Mr. Basketball—a large man able to power through and around other players.

Then, quickly, it dissolved into adversity.

His freshman season ended early when he broke his arm in a February 1996 car accident, as he and his teammates were heading back to Ann Arbor from a Detroit party at 5 a.m.

That crash kick-started the NCAA investigation that became the Martin scandal, getting Fisher fired, and sending the program into a devastating tailspin. Eventually, Traylor was among a group of players implicated for taking money from Martin, who steered him to Ann Arbor, and the big man was disassociated from the school for 10 years as part of the NCAA sanctions.

Banned from the University along with Chris Webber, Maurice Taylor, and Louis Bullock, Traylor became the exception, never getting a chance to reconnect with the school, as he died suddenly in 2011 from an apparent heart attack at age 34.

In his final years, he trotted the globe still playing basketball after heart surgery in 2006 made him too much of a risk for NBA teams to sign.

One of his former Michigan teammates from that 1998 group, Robbie Reid, called him "a true gentle giant" after hearing about Traylor's death.

Traylor's Michigan career was highlighted by moments worthy of his size—the backboard he accidentally shattered against Ball State as a sophomore, the NIT title, the fans swarming him on the Crisler court after the Duke upset.

But I'll remember that fearful moment in Chicago, when Purdue's Brad Miller—who went on to have a longtime NBA career—complained after the Wolverines' win in that Big Ten title game: "When you have that much weight on you, he's going to wear you down."

I had no interest in finding out.

Fortunately, Traylor passed over me and the others and into the stands, with no innocent college journalists flattened in his wake.

Traylor was Michigan's comet, a once-in-a-lifetime specimen of size and talent, unlikely to be replicated on the basketball court.

As my college career paralleled his (though we probably had a fair battle for fewest classes attended), I realize what a rare period that was.

Every game Traylor played was stricken from the University of Michigan record book as part of the NCAA sanctions, as if he never existed.

Anyone on campus from 1995 to 1998 would gladly dispute that notion, even if some of those moments—from a man that size moving in such a dynamic way—didn't seem real.

Mark Snyder started at the *Michigan Daily* in the fall of 1995 and stayed for four years, working as a sports editor as a senior in 1998 to 1999. During his *Daily* career he covered football, men's basketball, hockey, and softball. He was hired by the *Oakland Press* during his senior year and spent four years covering high school and Michigan State football before moving to the *Detroit Free Press*, where he has spent most of the past 10 years covering University of Michigan sports. He lives in Michigan with his wife and two kids.

ABOARD THE STRAIGHT TALK EXPRESS

JEREMY W. PETERS

February 2000

When I was hopping from state to state covering the 2012 presidential election for the *New York Times*, I would often think to myself, "Hey, I've done this before." I had indeed. Twelve years earlier when I was writing for the *Michigan Daily*, I had the good fortune of reporting on the historic 2000 election.

At that time, there were few better places to bear witness to presidential politics than Michigan. And as a young journalist with aspirations of traveling the campaign trail one day for a major news outlet, there were few better college papers to cut one's teeth than the *Michigan Daily*.

Michigan was one of the most contested states in 2000. Al Gore and George W. Bush visited it constantly. The contentious Republican primary that year between John McCain and Bush had one of its fiercest battles in Michigan. Ralph Nader even had a considerable campaign apparatus in the state—or at least it seemed that way from Ann Arbor. My *Daily* press pass gave me access to political figures I'd never dreamed of interviewing as someone who was so young I'd never even voted in a presidential election before.

I sat down at a reporters roundtable with Dick Cheney in suburban Detroit. I even put on a tie for the occasion. I lingered around after a Gore rally in Flint so I could snag a few quotes from his campaign manager, Donna Brazile. I waited at a rope line at one of Bush's town halls so I could shout a question at him. (He didn't answer.)

And as hanging chads were being counted in Florida, I traveled to

Washington to cover the first of two Supreme Court cases that would eventually settle the election in Bush's favor. I stood outside the court on a frigid December day as recordings of the oral arguments were replayed for those who weren't lucky enough to get inside.

But if there is one event from that year that really drove home the experience of being a campaign reporter, an adventure that bit me like a bug and left an indelible mark, it was covering McCain in the primary. To this day, I can look back at those few weeks and draw on lessons of resourcefulness and determination that remain with me.

This was the time when news often came by fax. Hot off the fax machine in the "bat cave," a dingy conference room tucked behind a set of small double doors just off the main newsroom, was a release from the College Republicans alerting us to a McCain event in Michigan. This was also the time when McCain had assumed the mantle of political maverick—as opposed to the various other iterations of his political persona like conservative curmudgeon or establishment Republican—and was therefore a natural draw for college students.

I jumped at the chance to go see McCain. But I had one problem: I wasn't guaranteed anything other than a glimpse of him at a campaign rally. I started to work every access channel I could think of. The College Republicans had a beef with the *Daily*, so they were no help. Chapters of local Republican Party committees were just as useless.

Luckily I had one last shot. During my internship the summer before at CNN, I had snagged a telephone directory that included the number of just about every presidential campaign operative a reporter would ever need. I flipped through it until I found the pages for the McCain campaign. I called a few numbers until someone told me where I could find the staffer who dealt with college media. Then after a few more phone calls I made my way to the spokesperson for his Michigan campaign. I left a message. Then another, and another after that.

The weekend campaign rally was quickly approaching, and I still hadn't heard back. Saturday rolled around, the day of the rally. I still didn't have my interview but decided to go anyway. As I was getting dressed and ready to hop into my University-loaned car, my cellphone buzzed. It was the spokesman I had been trying to reach all week. Much to my relief, he assured me I'd be able to spend a few minutes with McCain on his ubiquitous "Straight Talk Express" bus.

Sure enough, once I arrived at a hotel where McCain had stopped before the rally, I was ushered on board the bus and called to the back where I joined a group of reporters for the kind of impromptu roundtable I had read about McCain hosting all the time. Never did I think at that age I'd be part of one. I even got in a question or two. My experience resulted in a front-page story in the *Daily,* complete with a dateline that showed how little my editors and I could contain our excitement—"ABOARD THE STRAIGHT TALK EXPRESS." Just like it was a Navy vessel or something.

Someone far wiser than I told me once that you should look at journalism like a passport, a way to gain access to places and people that are beyond reach for most people. That's what covering the 2000 campaign for the *Daily* was like for me. It opened doors to a world I had always hoped to break into. And it's hard to imagine that I would be where I am today without those experiences.

Jeremy W. Peters was a reporter and news editor at the *Michigan Daily* from 1999 to 2002. After graduating in 2002, he spent the summer interning for the Detroit bureau of the *New York Times.* Warmer temperatures and the promise of a full-time job lured him to the U.S. Virgin Islands, where he spent two years as a reporter for the *Virgin Islands Daily News,* covering everything from corruption in the local government to carnival parades. The *New York Times* hired him back on a freelance basis in 2004 and made him a staff writer for the business desk in 2006. He has been with the *Times* since. His current beat is covering Congress. He lives in Washington, D.C.

9/11: THE VIEW FROM THE *DAILY*

GEOFFREY GAGNON

September 11, 2001

I took the stairs two at a time, turned quick at the old Coke machine and could hear the TV before I could see it. In the newsroom, a small group had formed a half circle in front of the temperamental old television. The room, big like a barn, was bright and mostly quiet. It felt early. The night before—a few hours ago, really—we had finished the paper late, wrapping a big story involving an athlete and a sexual assault. Everyone on campus would be talking about the news, we were sure of it.

Of course, they never did. On the morning of September 11, 2001, the newsroom was   swelling with *Daily* staffers who had no idea what was happening in New York. They crowded around the TV to see the towers of the World Trade Center ablaze with black smoke. By the time classes had been canceled, those buildings had vanished. Near Washington, the Pentagon was on fire too, and a plane had fallen to a field in Pennsylvania. We had no clue what it meant; no clue what it would come to mean later; and absolutely no clue what to put in the paper.

What was there for us to say? A reporter thought to call Robert Precht, a University law professor who had represented a defendant tried after the 1993 World Trade Center bombing. "Our society changes as of today," he explained without hesitation, echoing a sentiment that was quickly emerging. Pronouncements like these had a way of upping the ante on the matter that had loomed all afternoon: What to do with the front page? Like nearly everyone who comes to the *Daily*, we had worked in a kind of jealous awe of those predecessors who had seen

The Michigan Daily

NEWS: 76-DAILY
CLASSIFIED: 764-0557
www.michigandaily.com

One hundred ten years of editorial freedom

Ann Arbor, Michigan

Vol. CXI, No. 142

Wednesday
September 12, 2001

©2001 The Michigan Daily

America in crisis

'Our society changes as of today'

— Robert Precht
University Law professor and attorney for
1993 Trade Center bombing defendant

Flames burst from the south tower of the World Trade Center after a hijacked United Airlines 767 passenger jet slammed into the 110-story building shortly after another plane crashed into the north tower yesterday.

Trade Center collapses after attack

Students were left stunned, saddened and frantic to reach friends and family yesterday morning after a pair of hijacked airliners slammed into and demolished both towers of New York City's World Trade Center. The attack is the worst terrorist episode ever carried out in the United States.

Television stations carried live footage of the buildings' collapse, including pictures of a hijacked Boeing 757 slamming into the south tower. The attack began at about 8:45 a.m., and by 10:30 a.m. both buildings were absent from the city's skyline. In Washington, about 100 people died when a plane crashed into the Pentagon.

"Our society changes as of today. This is a watershed event," said Law Prof. Robert Precht, the attorney for one of the four men convicted of bombing the World Trade Center in 1993.

"I'm overwhelmed. I kind of wish I was back in the city — I can't reach my friends, the lines are down. I used to work down there, on the 82nd floor of the World Trade Center. ... I don't know if any of my co-workers actually survived," said Phillip Ng, an LSA sophomore from New York.

See ATTACK, Page 10

Inside coverage

Courtesy of the *Michigan Daily*.

some history—and had gotten the chance to record a bit of it in the paper. We pulled the big bound volumes down off the dusty shelves in the library, throwing open ancient editions of the *Daily*, and imagined ourselves at 420 Maynard Street after Pearl Harbor had been bombed, or after Kennedy had been killed. It seemed strange to wonder what September 11 might someday mean. Would anyone page through these big books to find tomorrow's paper?

Years removed, I marvel a bit at the confidence the *Daily* breeds. Sure, we worked for a mere campus newspaper, but we felt somehow immune to insignificance. This was the *Michigan Daily*, dammit. And so, with the country's airplanes grounded—and without a second thought—we packed reporters and photographers into cars pointed east. In the next days we ran stories from New York City, Washington, D.C., and Pennsylvania. Reliable Internet access was tougher—and costlier—in those days for a college reporter to locate, but we had help. In New York, where I reached a friend at Columbia University, our writers were invited to set up a quasi bureau at the *Columbia Daily Spectator*, from which they could file their stories back to Ann Arbor. When one of those pieces in particular arrived, more than a few eyes welled in the newsroom with tears.

It featured a simple and plaintive interview with a woman named Jill Gartenberg, who had met her husband Jim at an event for Michigan grads. Jim, who had been two years ahead of Jill in Ann Arbor, was the president of the alumni association's New York chapter, and when the two of them were married "The Victors" was played in the church. Jim worked in real estate, on the 86th floor of the North Tower of the World Trade Center. That's where he was on the morning of September 11. He was cleaning out his desk having recently accepted a new job in Midtown. Jill was pregnant with their second daughter. There was so much to be excited about.

The photo we ran to accompany the story of Jim and Jill Gartenberg showed their daughter, a toddler, who was dressed in maize and blue. "I say, 'What do you say when Daddy watches football?'" Jill said to a *Daily* reporter, looking at her daughter. "And she says, 'Go Blue!' He wanted those to be her first words."

By the end of the week, with plenty of stories to share and with Saturday's football game canceled, we tore up the weekend supplement typically circulated at the stadium and turned it instead into a special issue. It was exhilarating imagining what we could try. When two editors suggested that we should cover the burgeoning American military response by sending a reporter to Afghanistan and Pakistan, it somehow seemed sensible. The three-part series that followed concerned the tricky geopolitics of the region and, I admit, represented something of a contrast to, say, our women's soccer coverage that week.

Later, a member of the Board for Student Publications, which keeps tabs on the paper's finances, peered over the rims of his glasses to grumble about the lost photo equipment that I'd reported. I'm sure I smiled when I had to recount the story of how the border guards in Pakistan had been unkind to our reporter and seized the *Daily*'s pricey camera. "Oh yeah," I explained with feigned authority, "that stretch of the border can get a little dicey." I had no clue what I was talking about and mumbled something about history! Of course, the members of the board must have understood it. I think some of them—those who had worked at the *Daily* and remembered the big story that landed on their watch—must have appreciated, even better than I did then, the paper's near magical propensity to awaken a spirit of possibility. This was the *Michigan Daily*, dammit.

The next month, I sat in the library at the *Daily* with a couple of editors from *Newsweek*. In those days of yore, the magazine was still a venerated arbiter of the national zeitgeist and had sent a team to Ann Arbor to survey the rippling effects of September 11 on America's young people. In a cover story that proclaimed us all a part of "Generation 9-11," the magazine highlighted the *Daily*'s coverage over those heady weeks that fall. As for the years ahead, the magazine predicted war, political upheaval, and profound uncertainty. My own uncertainty had less to do with September 11, than with the hardly unique mystery of what to do after college. When that subject had come up with the friendly women from *Newsweek*, I explained that I was headed to law school—or something like that. Maybe. No, definitely.

Before flying back to New York, one of the editors asked if I'd ever thought of magazines. I hadn't. Not about working for one, anyway. I wasn't even sure how. The idea sounded amazing, but the path was so unclear. Still, we stayed in touch. And months later, after graduation, I swung by her book-lined office to say hello the morning I started an internship at *Newsweek*. In the weeks that followed, as I caught a glimpse of what a career in magazines might look like, I thought a lot about the *Daily*, and about the things there that always felt possible. And I was reminded of our long day at the paper, and the uneasy days that came next, when I saw my first big magazine story appear in *Newsweek*—a piece about the first anniversary of the 9/11 attacks.

Geoffrey Gagnon joined the *Michigan Daily* as a sports reporter in 1998 and served as editor-in-chief in 2001. Today he is articles editor at *GQ* magazine. Previously he was editorial director at *Politico Magazine*, which he helped launch, and was senior editor at the *Atlantic* in Washington, D.C. He also served as senior editor at *Boston* magazine and was managing editor at *Legal Affairs* magazine. He lives in New York City.

COVERING A UNIVERSITY ON TRIAL

SHANNON PETTYPIECE

2002

I walked into the *Michigan Daily* for the first time on a cold Sunday morning in 2001. I didn't know a thing about journalism and wasn't much of a writer. I was mostly just looking for an extracurricular activity where I could make friends, and a student newspaper seemed like as good a place as any.

But, if you've ever had a job on a newspaper, you'll know that's just not how it works. A year later I was spending the majority of my time at the paper, helping to cover a historic legal battle over the consideration of race in college admissions. The case over the University of Michigan's use of affirmative action became an emotionally, politically, and intellectually complex story that the entire country was watching. And here I was, a 20-year-old with just a few stories under my belt, on the frontlines. I was thrust into covering a topic I knew nothing about, but that didn't mean I'd get any slack if I got it wrong.

Starting to write for the *Daily* is like being thrown into the deep end of the pool. There was no formal training. I spent a few hours shadowing another reporter on my first day and on my second day was handed a story and sent on my way.

You learned from your mistakes and from the editors, who themselves had been thrown in just a few years before you. During my junior year, I was picked by the editors to cover the University's administration, which included following the affirmative action case. Covering this legal battle was a torch that had been passed from one class of reporters to the next since the University was sued in 1997. One of the suits involved two students denied admission to the College of Literature, Science, and the Arts, while a separate lawsuit was filed by a law school applicant.

By the time I got my hands on the story, in 2002, one judge had ruled in favor of affirmative action in the LSA case and another judge ruled against its use at the law school. Both sides appealed the rulings, and the issue was now in the hands of the justices on the federal Sixth Circuit Court of Appeals.

My job was to prepare for when the ruling came down so that I could explain the implications and significance of the decision—whichever way it went—to the tens of thousands of students on campus.

The wonderful thing about being a reporter at Michigan is that there is no shortage of sources to help understand issues, however complex. Many University professors were happy to help answer the most basic questions and provide legal background. I even had the guidance of a former Supreme Court reporter, Anthony Collings, who was teaching a course on media coverage of the high court.

As the University waited for a decision from the court, much of the news that filled the *Daily*'s pages revolved around the heated debate over race that was boiling on campus. There were rallies on the Diag and the steps of the Union by groups for and against—both sides shouting, chanting, pushing fliers in students' hands. At the *Daily*, we had to balance the coverage, deciding when a rally merited an article and how we would avoid becoming just a mouthpiece for either side. We also had to figure out how to deal with the criticism that came our way, however we told the story.

The division over the case was also playing out at the highest levels of the University administration, and on a March afternoon, it became public. I received an anonymous piece of mail at the *Daily*. Inside was a copy of a letter from Republican Regent Daniel Horning to Democratic Regent Kathy White.

In the letter, Horning wrote to White that her objections to having two white males as chair and vice chair of the Board of Regents "reek of everything wrong with affirmative action."

He went on to say that while he publicly supported the University's use of affirmative action, he was personally opposed to it.

In the letter he wrote, "I would like to invite you to join me the next time I visit with a high school senior and his/her parents to explain why a 3.85 GPA and 30 ACT score just aren't enough for the University of Michigan . . . even with a letter of recommendation from a sitting regent . . . Can you imagine me explaining that if they were a minority or from an underrepresented group of people it would be acceptable but being a Caucasian from western Michigan creates a problem?"

I never learned who sent me the letter or why, and I don't even really have a good guess, but Horning's position was significant not only because it showed the infighting going on behind closed doors at the top of the University, but because it raised the question of whether the Regents would continue to support affirmative action admissions. Regardless of whether the University won its legal challenges, the Regents could decide at any point to remove race from admissions decisions.

The story landed on the front page and was followed up several days later by an apology from Horning, who retracted what he said in the letter.

A month before the Supreme Court handed down a split ruling in June 2003—upholding the law school's use of affirmative action while striking down use for undergraduate applicants—I had graduated and started my first job as a reporter in Miami. I watched the coverage play out in the *Daily* by the reporters I helped train as an editor and hoped I'd done a good job passing on the torch.

Today, *Daily* reporters are still covering the story. While I was writing this piece, the Supreme Court upheld Michigan's ban on using affirmative action in admissions at public colleges, renewing the debate on campus over what role race should play in admissions.

Ten years later, as a reporter for Bloomberg News, I found myself once again covering a complex and politically charged issue before the nation's highest courts. This time it was President Barack Obama's health care law. As I prepared for the ruling to come down, I thought about what I'd learned in my time at the *Daily* and realized that while I now had thousands of stories under my belt and was writing for a national audience, there aren't too many differences between covering a story from the nation's capital or 420 Maynard.

Shannon Pettypiece was a reporter and news editor for the *Michigan Daily* from 2001 to 2003. After leaving the *Daily* she interned for the *New York Times* in Detroit and worked as a business reporter in Miami and Cleveland. She is currently a special projects reporter at Bloomberg News with a focus on covering health care. In addition to writing for the Bloomberg terminal and Bloomberg.com, she contributes to Bloomberg TV, Bloomberg Radio, and *Businessweek* magazine. She's also appeared as a guest for multiple programs on CBS, CNN, MSNBC, ABC, NPR, and PBS. She currently lives in New York with her husband and son.

THE GAME THAT NEVER OCCURRED

CHRIS BURKE

November 7, 2002

Chris Webber's infamous timeout in the 1993 national championship game was a defining moment of my childhood. So much so, in fact, that when time came to apply to the University of Michigan, I used part of the required essay to recall how my heartbroken 10-year-old self cried alone in his bedroom after that loss.

Imagine my surprise then on the morning of November 7, 2002, as I sat inside a room at the Michigan Union with my colleagues on the *Daily*'s basketball beat and listened as University President Mary Sue Coleman essentially declared that game never occurred.

The men's basketball program had cheated, Coleman said, so the Wolverines would forfeit that classic '93 title game, as well as the previous year's trip to the championship round and more than 100 other contests spanning parts of six seasons. Shortly before the press conference began, we later learned, the banners celebrating two Final Fours, an NIT championship, and a Big Ten Tournament title were dragged unceremoniously from the Crisler Center rafters, to be tucked away in storage like the Ark of the Covenant in *Indiana Jones.*

And just like that, Michigan's hoops history had been rewritten.

"There is no excuse for what happened. It was wrong, plain and simple," Coleman said. "We have let down all who believe that the University of Michigan should stand for the best in college athletics. We have disappointed our students, our faculty, our alumni, and our fans. This is a day of great shame for the University."

"I am determined that nothing like this will ever happen again at Michigan."

It felt like a funeral, with Coleman delivering the eulogy. In fact, the next day's *Michigan Daily* included a tombstone graphic that read: "GONE BUT NOT FORGOTTEN" and featured the dates of every forfeited game.

Keep in mind, too, that this took place a mere three months into Coleman's tenure as president, which lasted until 2014. For many Michigan students, fans, and casual observers, this was the first real exposure to Coleman. The basketball sanctions lingered on her résumé for the duration of her time in Ann Arbor.

"When I realized what I was going to say today, this was very tough," said Coleman, sounding genuinely heartbroken. "When I looked at the basketball media guide, I realized that it was going to change. This was really hard. We are embarrassed because this is not what Michigan is all about. This has been a big impact, but it is relief too. We now have a bright future with a great coach and great young people. You are going to be proud again of Michigan."

Apparently, the only way to protect the Wolverines' future, at least in the eyes of the new regime, was to (attempt to) erase the past.

Erased from the record books were the only two seasons that the quintet of Webber, Jalen Rose, Juwan Howard, Jimmy King, and Ray Jackson played together—two of the most remarkable, memorable, groundbreaking seasons in the history of college basketball. How many basketball players in the decade between the Fab Five's arrival in Ann Arbor and Coleman's announcement had cultivated their love of the game while watching Webber and his mates swagger their way around the world? What percentage of new Michigan students in the mid-to-late 90's began dreaming of wearing the Maize and Blue after reveling in the Fab Five's baggy shorts, black shoes, and overall disdain for authority?

Plain and simple, the Fab Five had changed the entire culture of college basketball. There may never again be another collection of teammates so perfectly built for the national TV stage, so intrinsically entertaining no matter the opponent or score or setting.

Webber was the centerpiece, a do-everything forward with the vision of a point guard and the brashness of an NBA Hall of Famer.

In the end, his presence also served as a major player in the program's undoing. Webber allegedly was the biggest beneficiary of loans from ex-booster Ed Martin to multiple Wolverine basketball stars—Maurice Taylor, Robert Traylor, Louis Bullock, and the others named in the case.

Michigan tried to escape the situation multiple times. In 1996, after Traylor and Bullock (among others) were involved in a car accident, the University revealed an NCAA fraction. Pushed to investigate further, Michigan found two more minor infractions. Less than a year later, head basketball coach Steve Fisher was let go. His replacement, Brian Ellerbe, was pushed out in 2001.

There were other factors at play—poor on-court performance and dwindling attendance, to name a couple—but the specter of the Ed Martin case refused to vanish.

Almost everyone accepted there was more punishment to come before Coleman took to the podium, after the NCAA three weeks earlier had delivered an official letter of inquiry into Michigan's basketball program. Still, the verdict was a rather shocking one. Not only did Michigan throw head coach Tommy Amaker and his players in the line of fire by placing them on two years of postseason probation, it attempted to wash its hands of some of the most storied years in the program's history.

The reactions, not surprisingly, ran the gamut.

Coleman and Martin sounded apologetic, even if they never specifically expressed it. Amaker praised the maturity with which his team handled the news. The students, past and present, were furious.

Personally, the situation marked a crash course in how unique the coverage situation is at the *Daily*. I knew that making the switch from student and Maize Rager to basketball reporter during my third year with the paper was going to be an adjustment—one I mimicked a year earlier to cover Red Berenson's hockey team. But I also entered into the assignment with the romantic notion in the back of my head that I might be there for Michigan's return to the NCAA Tournament.

The very short walk from the Union back to the *Daily*'s newsroom allowed me an opportunity to regroup. When I was home, chatting with my roommates, I could vent a bit about the basketball program's misfortune. As it often did throughout my extended five-year stay in college, though, the paper came first.

So, I called up former Athletic Director Don Canham.

"I think what they did was exactly right and exactly what they had to do," Canham said. "I really don't know what the hell the NCAA Infractions Committee could do in addition. (The committee added—then later rescinded—a second year of probation).

"Anyone who looks at the violations probably understands that this is the worst violation in the history of college basketball. What Fisher has done to the basketball program and the University because he's incompetent is beyond belief. I don't think he cheated, but he's incompetent. It's a shame to see such a great basketball program ruined by incompetence."

Strong words to help put the situation in perspective, but also further evidence of the difficulty in the immediate aftermath. Steve Fisher already was several seasons into his tenure as head coach at San Diego State, with no further punishment outside of previously losing the Michigan job. Webber, Taylor, and Traylor were in the NBA; Bullock was playing overseas.

What also really stood out about the sanctions: No story I covered during my brief *Daily* time before, nor anything I have covered since, had the staying power this story did. By the time Coleman summoned the media for this press conference, the tale had been unfolding for a decade.

Did it ever stop?

The season that coincided with the sanctions was an unstoppable whirlwind. When the Wolverines came out of the gate 0-6, the reasoning read that they were too crushed by not having anything to play for; when they subsequently ran off 13-straight wins to enter the Big Ten race, it only stood to reason they were drawing strength from an "us against the world" situation. Two years later, when Amaker and Michigan won the NIT, the celebration focused on putting a legit banner in the Crisler rafters to replace those missing.

Even when Amaker's stay in Ann Arbor crumbled amid several disappointing seasons and John Beilein took over the coaching post, talk often circled back to moving the program past its prior humiliation.

There was no denying how lasting the black eye was on Michigan's Athletic Department, one that prides itself on paying homage to tradition. Imagine the football program omitting Lloyd Carr's contributions or the hockey program blacklisting the names of Brendan Morrison or Marty Turco.

Those comparisons may not even do justice to what was lost on the court. The Fab Five changed the athletic world, and the group that came after them—including Taylor, Traylor, and Bullock—lived in their wake.

By about 10:15 a.m. on that November day in 2002, they all were nothing more than memories.

Chris Burke was a member of the *Daily* sports staff from 2000 to 2005 (he was unofficially granted a redshirt season). In college, he also worked as a blogger for MLive's Michigan sports page. After leaving the Ann Arbor area, he became a sportswriter for the *Fauquier Times-Democrat* and later was promoted to sports editor at the *Culpeper Times*, both located in Virginia. In 2008, he was hired by AOL Sports, where he eventually took charge of an NFL editor role. *Sports Illustrated* brought him on in 2011 as an NFL writer, which remains his current position.

ONE SEASON, TWO RECEIVERS AND FINDING A CAREER IN JOURNALISM

J. BRADY MCCOLLOUGH

Fall 2003

I am sitting in an airport, clicking through my phone, passing the time until boarding. If I look bored to you, well, you've incorrectly read the situation. I am heading back to Pittsburgh, Pennsylvania, where a newspaper actually pays me to do nothing but write sports features. I am loving life. Seriously. I just finished what is probably the best story of my career, a four-part series that deals with the remarkable challenges faced by kids with mental health issues, using basketball as the narrative vehicle. I feel as if I have been working toward that story for a solid decade. A month from now, I will go to Russia to cover the 2014 Sochi Olympics, to write about some of the best athletes in the world as they accomplish their lifelong dreams. I do not say all of this to be boastful. I say it to show my gratitude. It is truly one of those days.

And I am not shocked at all, when I look up to the flat-screen TV that's hanging at the gate, to see Jason Avant making a catch for the Philadelphia Eagles against the Dallas Cowboys.

When I reflect on the direction of my journalism career post–*Michigan Daily*, it is hard not to think about Jason Avant. And I can't think about Jason Avant without also pondering Braylon Edwards.

Most of you won't need much of an introduction to Braylon and Jason. They were Michigan football wide receivers, great in ways that couldn't have been more different. Braylon's talent was undeniable, sometimes awe-inspiring. Jason's work ethic had been molded by the women who raised him on the South Side of Chicago and was equally special.

They would share the plush green field in back-to-back Rose Bowls and have their day in the NFL. But before that, a 21-year-old with aspirations of becoming a sportswriter was forced to observe them, consider them, and make decisions on how to portray them to a captive student body. Let's not forget, Jason and Braylon were technically fellow students. And, despite my bravado, I had no idea what I was doing. Of course, that was the beauty of the *Michigan Daily*. In the asbestos-ridden first floor of 420 Maynard where the sports staff toiled and laughed the nights away, it was up to me and me alone to figure it out.

When choosing a university to attend, a lot of kids include a big-time sports experience on their list of wants. But I'm not sure many of them go to the lengths that I did to make sure I was going to love attending my future alma mater's football games.

I was down to the University of Texas and the University of Michigan. How would I decide without going to a football game at each place? Somehow, my parents understood me enough to get it. In August of 1999, my dad took me to the Texas–North Carolina State game in Austin. I tried to imagine myself in jeans and cowboy boots and burnt orange, and I felt pretty good about it. A week later, my mom took me to the Michigan–Notre Dame game in Ann Arbor. A guy named Tom Brady led the Wolverines on a game-winning drive in the fourth quarter, and if I were a player and this was my recruitment, I would have given Lloyd Carr and the Wolverines my verbal commitment right then and there.

Receiving my admission letter from Michigan was one of the most exciting moments of my 18 years. Once there, I thought I would major in something practical, like math or statistics, and I took all of those classes. In those halls of learning, I would read the *Michigan Daily* sports section and sit there amazed that these students got to cover the football team I throatily cheered on Saturdays. They got to ask Coach Carr questions? Hold his feet to the fire for his conservatism?

My friends in South Quad knew that I wanted to write for the *Daily*. Finally, one of them challenged me to stop talking and walk through that door. I went to the Sunday sports meeting in late January 2001 and was assigned a football recruiting story and coverage of a women's track meet. I would never stop walking through that door.

By the start of my junior year, I had earned one of the four coveted spots on the Michigan football beat at the *Daily*. During that season, Braylon

Edwards had emerged as one of the top wide receivers in the Big Ten, and going into the next year, he had made the bold request to wear the No. 1 jersey, the one worn by Anthony Carter, Derrick Alexander, and David Terrell, the one that signified that he was the man.

And Lloyd Carr gave it to him, a show of faith. But with the No. 1 jersey came expectations and extra scrutiny. So when Carr made it very clear that Edwards was in his doghouse in late September of the 2003 season, after the Wolverines had lost at Oregon, I felt it was my job to find out what was going on.

The next week against Indiana at the Big House, Edwards did not play early in the game. Carr was trying to send him a message. After the game, I waited for Edwards outside the locker room. While I waited, I ran into his father, Stan Edwards, who had been a star running back at Michigan under Bo Schembechler. Stan pulled no punches when talking about his son and essentially said Braylon needed to grow up. I had a good column right there, but I still wanted to give Braylon a chance to respond. I knew that I would have wanted the same courtesy if someone were about to write a column about me for nearly 40,000 students to read.

When Braylon walked out and I asked him for a quick interview, he blew me off. "Not today, not today," he said.

I wasn't surprised. And if I didn't have the strong words from his father, I probably would have had weak grounds for a column that called out Braylon Edwards for not respecting the No. 1 jersey. But the next day when I sat down to write the SportsMonday column, I let him have it. It was probably the most scathing thing I wrote at the *Daily* and possibly since.

How much did I embarrass him in the *Daily*? I compared him to R. Kelly.

It was not an easy column to write. At my core, I am not confrontational. I want people to like me. But to be a journalist—and that is what I had decided to be—I had to be able to take a stand and stick by it. If Braylon's father could say it, so could I.

A few weeks later, Braylon's performance improved, and he was back in Carr's good graces. As Michigan began to turn its season around on the way to a Rose Bowl berth, the Athletic Department made Edwards available to media at one of the weekly press conferences. I wasn't there (I must have had a school conflict or something), but I would later hear that Braylon had mentioned me by name and said that he had read the column and did not like the way he was portrayed, that he wanted to show people that he was a good guy. Later, after Michigan won at Michigan State in early November, I wrote a column that gave Edwards credit for turning his season around.

The next year, he'd return to school for his senior year and win the Biletnikoff Award, given to the nation's top wide receiver, and, accurate or not, I felt I may have had something to do with it.

Jason Avant lived in Braylon Edwards' shadow for two seasons, but his story caught my attention. We were talking just the two of us after a weekly press conference, and he told me about how his grandmother raised him on the gritty South Side of Chicago because his mother and father were not in his life.

It was not a totally unique story, in retrospect. Sadly, stuff like that happens all the time. But to me, at 21 years old, Jason Avant's story was the most interesting thing I'd run into in my journalism career. What was that like for him? How did he come from that neighborhood under those circumstances and make it to the University of Michigan? For the first time, instead of reporting a feature story by making phone calls, I would go to the South Side to see for myself.

Michigan was playing at Northwestern in mid-November 2003, and so I planned with a *Daily* photographer to go there a few days early to speak with Jason's grandmother, Lilly, and aunt, and his high school coach at Carver High School. Lilly Avant's health wasn't good, but she was able to focus long enough to tell me her grandson's story.

"Children need their mother," she'd repeat. "Children need their mother."

Jason's mother had left him at Lilly's doorstep when he was just a toddler. Now that Lilly had raised him into a college student and football star, Jason's mother was trying to get back into his life. He was trying to reopen himself to her. The story was heartbreaking and uplifting all at the same time, like all the best ones.

That piece would be the best thing I wrote at the *Daily*. It very well could have gotten me one of my internships or first job. It was always the first story in my package of clips. And it showed a totally different side of the journalist I was going to be than that column on Braylon Edwards.

Each year, it seemed the Philadelphia Eagles couldn't put together a roster without Jason Avant. He was the same guy he always had been at

Michigan—tough, dependable, willing to do whatever it takes to stay on the field, including playing special teams. But last offseason, after eight years, the Eagles let him go. Still, their comments showed how tough it was for them to part ways—and how easy it would be for him to find another team.

"There have not been any players who have represented the Philadelphia Eagles with more class and dignity than Jason Avant," Eagles team chairman Jeffrey Lurie said in a statement. "Whether it was in the locker room, on the playing field, or in the community, he has always been a true professional, a role model, and a winner every step of the way."

In 2013, Braylon Edwards was looking for work. He had been drafted No. 3 overall by the Cleveland Browns, guaranteed millions of dollars, and he had squandered all of it. He made one Pro Bowl, in 2007, but could not stay out of trouble off the field (he's had numerous assault charges against him and also a charge of driving under the influence) and was seen as a head case around the league.

I don't want to say that my judgment of him at 21 years old was right, because it's not about that. Frankly, it's sad that he never was able to put aside his ego and become the player he could have been—especially because, during Braylon's last three years at Michigan, he had the perfect role model standing right beside him.

Most young sportswriters want to be columnists. I know I did. Your face is out there, and it's obvious to everyone that the words and the space are yours. As a sports columnist, you can become famous, a household name. What 21-year-old doesn't want that?

There was a rush that came with that column on Edwards, and all the columns that I wrote at the *Daily*. There was a rush that came with being recognized on campus, at class, or at a party.

But nothing compared to the feeling of knowing somebody else's story so intimately that you could confidently share it with the world. There was a trust there, between subject and writer, that felt sacred and special. And ever since I left the South Side of Chicago, I have been constantly looking for that feeling.

A great column can be thought-provoking and change-inducing. Maybe I'll get the chance to do it again in the future. If not, I'm OK with that. Because there is nothing more powerful than a well-told story, and I learned that by covering football at the *Michigan Daily*.

J. Brady McCollough was a reporter and sports editor at the *Michigan Daily* from 2000 to 2003, holding the role of managing sports editor his last year. After graduating in 2004, he interned at the *Dallas Morning News* and began working at the *Kansas City Star* in 2005. At the *Star*, he covered the University of Kansas Athletic Department for five years, including the 2008 basketball national championship team and 2010 ticket scandal that resulted in the federal indictment of several KU employees. In 2012, he moved on to the *Pittsburgh Post-Gazette* to write sports features and enterprise stories. He has covered the Olympics in London and Sochi and is very much looking forward to Rio de Janeiro in 2016.

"LIBERATING" VANDY CHAIRS

TONY DING

December 6, 2003

A college institution like the *Michigan Daily* boasts many unique collegiate traditions, and the fruits of one of these still sits proudly on display in my living room—a black, padded-vinyl folding chair emblazoned with the Vanderbilt University logo. Now why would a Wolverine keep a Vandy chair? That will more so require explaining *how* I came upon it, on a weekend trip to the country music capital of the world my junior year.

I flew in from Detroit with two *Daily* sportswriters to cover the Michigan men's basketball team's non-conference ACC–Big Ten Challenge bout with Vanderbilt. We stayed at a Holiday Inn right on campus, and literally adjacent to the basketball arena. Very convenient.

The game was a foregone conclusion, as Michigan was still very much in the midst of its rebuilding era and duly outmatched by Vanderbilt. After the game, we worked at a leisurely pace, since we weren't publishing the paper until Monday morning and weren't on deadline. I found myself the last photog left in the small windowless photographer's workroom in the bowels of the arena, and the writers were still out at their courtside seats. Wandering out of the workroom intending to encourage my colleagues to finish up, I happened upon a storage room with the door open. Inside were a few folding chairs. They were identical to Vanderbilt's bench chairs courtside, except those were chained together, and these were unattended.

Without thinking, I decided to liberate two of the chairs, grabbing one in each hand, and instinctively bolted for the nearest exit. I realized I couldn't just stroll out of the arena through the concourse gates. An arena janitor or other facility person would surely be suspicious. So, I ventured to a nearby stairwell, and upon seeing an emergency exit that didn't appear to have an alarm, opened the door. Silence. Relieved, I found that the emergency exit opened out to the side of the arena, along a perimeter sidewalk alley lined with a thick hedge. Standing in the doorway without stepping outside, I chucked both chairs into the leafy row of bushes.

My writer colleagues were a bit confused when I told them what happened, as we calmly and quietly walked out of the arena through the main entrance. They quickly saw the brilliance of the coup though, as we nonchalantly retrieved the two chairs I had deposited in the hedges. Sneaking unseen back to our quiet hotel room nearby was uneventful, as the darkness shaded us. What developed next, however, was the most ingenious innovation of our challenge.

Since we flew to Nashville and were flying back to Detroit that next morning, we couldn't just hand-carry two folding chairs onto the plane, even if they didn't have the Vanderbilt logo emblazoned loudly on the chair backs. So, after a bit of brainstorming in our hotel room and flipping through the hotel phonebook (yes yellow pages still existed!), the three of us walked to a nearby Kinkos store. I can't recall if we paid for or were able to simply get a free bunch of brown butcher paper, 3 feet wide, and some tape, with which we returned to the hotel and wrapped up the two folding chairs, so they became two perfectly unidentifiable rectangular packages.

You can probably guess the rest. And yes, we felt smug and wore ridiculously smug grins the whole flight home. Sure, the Delta baggage check agent gave us some odd looks at the Nashville airport, but this was before airlines charged for checked luggage, so it wasn't that out of the question a couple of college kids wanted to check two pieces of "furniture" on a flight. The agent tagged 'em, and down the conveyor belt they went!

I wasn't the first *Daily* staffer to "liberate" a souvenir with an away school's name when on a road trip—someone once brought back a framed photo lifted from Beaver Stadium in the 90's—but I did reinvigorate the trend, and my Vandy chair went on to inspire other untold booty begotten in the name of *Daily* tradition.

Tony Ding joined the *Michigan Daily* in 2002 as an arts writer reviewing alternative pop punk albums and concerts. After photos taken at a Green Day concert impressed the photo editor, he was poached to be a staff photographer and ultimately served as managing photo editor from 2003 to 2005. After graduating, he has continued to work in Michigan as a freelance photographer with The Associated Press, having covered every season of Michigan football and basketball the last decade. He also regularly shoots the Detroit Red Wings, Michigan State basketball, and the occasional Tigers, Lions, and Pistons games. Outside of sports, he has covered the auto industry, elections, riots, and has shot/ate his way through a *New York Times* "36 Hours in Ann Arbor" feature. He lives in Ann Arbor.

LITTLE BROTHER, BIG RIVALRY

SCOTT BELL

Michigan–Michigan State Week
2005, 2006, and 2007

I can't even begin to list the amount of incredible opportunities you're afforded when you become a member of the *Michigan Daily* staff. You get the chance to grow as a student, as a journalist, and as a person during your handful of years spent calling 420 Maynard home. You're given the chance to work alongside some of the region and nation's best journalists, covering the same high-profile events that they are. And because of the *Daily*'s great reputation, you're treated like one of their peers. You're treated like a professional, because at the *Daily,* you learn to become one.

But then there's Michigan–Michigan State week. And everything mentioned in that glowing opening paragraph goes right out the window.

It's the one sliver of the year when instead of just writing about games, you're also participating in one. And it's the one week of the year when you're going out of your way to write something you *hope* upsets a large number of people.

So what is it about Michigan–Michigan State week that leads a handful of journalists to briefly look the other way when it comes to professionalism and impartiality? What makes a week so special that it often leads to a war of words . . . and sometimes a little more? Here's a peek behind the curtain at the week's two key elements—the dueling columns and the *Daily–State News* football game.

Dueling Columns

Each year, one *Daily* sportswriter is given the opportunity to "collaborate" with a Michigan State student. You're instructed to pen a column that's basically designed to say why your school and your school's football team are superior. Cheap shots are not only allowed, they're encouraged.

The catch: You're not only writing for the *Daily* audience—the column also appears in Michigan State's student newspaper, the *State News*, which is distributed throughout the Spartan campus.

How do I know that Spartan fans read them? Well, in 2006, when I made my debut as the *Daily*'s dueling columnist, I got 147 emails from Spartan fans who didn't exactly see eye-to-eye with my point of view. These messages ranged from "you're not as funny as you think you are" to "you should be expelled." Ninety-nine percent of the time, if you're a journalist waking up to an inbox clogged with angry messages, you've failed. But during Michigan–Michigan State week, those emails are all little trophies in my book.

My personal (printable) favorite response came from a gentleman named Nick who said he and "60 drunken frat guys" would spend their Saturday solely looking for me. An unedited excerpt:

"You did yourself a great disservice by writing that clever article Scotty because now I think you have every student at State wanting to drive down there just to see you. We know we're going to lose and thats the beauty of it all. We just don't care. We'd rather drive down there and get black out drunk and search for your scrawny little ass. Have a great Saturday Scotty. You're going to spend it dodging drunken State fans all day and if one of us find you, good luck."

Spoiler alert: They didn't find me. But some Michigan State students who happened to be tailgating next to me and my friends the day of the Michigan–Michigan State game did show up with newspapers that had my headshot next to my column so they could "find the idiot who wrote this." But all threats proved empty, and I remained in one piece.

The next year, my senior year, I once again got to write the dueling column. (True story: At the beginning of football season, *Daily* sportswriters typically position themselves as best they can to get to write the marquee stories for big games. But while my colleagues were arguing to write the game column for Ohio State or the big story for Notre Dame week, my No. 1 choice was the dueling column for Michigan State week. I regret nothing.)

During my dueling column in 2007, I referred to Michigan State fans as "little brother." The previous year, I had referred to Michigan State as "the annoying little sibling who always wants attention."

Following the 2007 game, in which Michigan won 28–24 after a dramatic comeback, Michigan running back Mike Hart made his now infamous "little brother" comments in the post-game press conference. Now, I certainly don't want to take credit for an iconic moment in the Michigan–Michigan State rivalry or anything, but let's just say I've been told Mr. Hart was a frequent reader of the *Daily* . . .

All in all, it's really just a welcome change of pace. When the next Monday rolls around and Michigan State week is in your rear view mirror, it's right back to the world of breaking news, player interviews, and writing fair, balanced pieces.

But in a field where you can have a tendency to take yourself way too seriously, the annual dueling column is a welcome opportunity to be a little reckless and have a lot of fun.

The *Daily–State News* Game

Not-so-breaking news: Journalists aren't always the most athletic people in the world. But hey, that doesn't stop them from having fun.

The "main event" of *Daily–State News* week is the *Daily–State News* game—a perfect way to punctuate a week that's fueled by equal parts anticipation and antagonization.

While the dueling columns may be an entertaining way to fire up both campuses, the *Daily–State News* game is what most staff members look forward to, because unlike the column, anyone can participate.

A quick rundown of the game itself:

Members of the *Daily* staff take on members of the *State News* staff in a football game the night before each school's actual team plays. It's 8-on-8, with a minimum of two girls on the field at all time. All sections of the paper are welcome. Two-hand touch*. First team to 10 touchdowns wins.

(Two-hand touch gets an asterisk, because at some point in almost every game, things get a little testy and extend a little beyond the two-hand touch parameters.)

I'm hardly an expert on the Ann Arbor economy, but I'm pretty confident that eye black vendors and barbers who cut mohawks look forward to the *Daily–State News* game almost as much as the participants.

Put it this way: If you were playing in the *Daily–State News* game and you *didn't* have eye black on, you probably stood out just as much as someone would if he or she wore eye black to class.

On more than one occasion, the game has gotten a shoutout during the telecast of the actual Michigan–Michigan State game with some B-roll footage of the previous night's game. Area newspapers and television stations have sent reporters to capture the scene. It really is a sight to behold.

As I'm writing this now, the *Daily* is currently on a 10-game winning streak. But since you may be reading this many years down the line, I've provided you with this helpful math problem to let you know where the *Daily*'s streak currently sits. Because let's be honest: The *State News* isn't going to be winning anytime soon.

[Current year] − 2004 = [*Daily*'s current win streak]

So what spurred the *Daily*'s current winning streak? Well, it all started with The Flag Game.

A few weeks before the 2005 game, Michigan State and Notre Dame's actual teams had faced off in South Bend. The Spartans won a 44–41 thriller in overtime. Following the win, a bunch of Spartans took the Michigan State flag and planted it at midfield of the Fighting Irish's turf. It grabbed national headlines.

Some found it to be funny. Others thought it was disrespectful. But to the *Daily* staff, it was something completely different—it was inspiring.

Two short weeks later, on the eve of Michigan and Michigan State facing off at Spartan Stadium, the *Daily* and *State News* teams squared off in East Lansing. The game itself wasn't particularly dramatic or intriguing: The *Daily* won comfortably, 10–3.

Following the post-game tradition of completing empty, half-assed handshakes, a group from the *Daily* decided to pull out a Michigan flag that we just happened to bring to the game and plant it at midfield.

Classy? Not so much. But memorable? Absolutely.

It's those memorable moments that make this game so great. Some preceded The Flag Game, like in 1994, when players from both teams went to the hospital, and carnage was so bad that the 1995 game was canceled. Other unforgettable moments have happened since, like the double-overtime thriller in 2010 that ended in a 10–9 victory for the *Daily*.

No matter which memorable moment you prefer, you're bound to collect a handful of them during your four years as a member of the *Daily*. For me, those moments were defined by covering hirings and firings and everything in between. I got to cover the 2007 Rose Bowl and basketball games at Madison Square Garden. I was even fortunate enough to cover a national championship (hey, it was softball, but it still counts).

I'm truly indebted to the *Daily* for all these incredible experiences, and I'm fully aware I wouldn't be anywhere near the journalist I am today without them.

But it's the traditions like those during Michigan–Michigan State week that highlight just how great the whole *Daily* experience is. As dumb and cliché as it sounds, the sense of camaraderie the *Daily–State News* game creates extends to the newsroom, which goes on to extend to some lifelong friendships.

Not a bad byproduct for a silly little game of touch football.

Scott Bell was a reporter, columnist, and managing sports editor at the *Michigan Daily* from 2004 to 2008. After graduating in 2008, he joined the *Detroit Free Press*, first as an intern, then as a full-time staffer for the sports section. In 2010, he turned in his winter coat for cowboy boots and took a job as online assistant sports editor for the *Dallas Morning News*, where he oversaw day-to-day digital operations for SportsDay, the *Morning News'* award-winning sports section. In 2013, he was promoted to assistant sports editor. In that role, he manages the paper's NBA Mavericks, NHL Stars, high school sports, and soccer coverage. He resides in McKinney, Texas.

A STREAK OF BAD *DAILY* SPORTS LUCK

NICOLE AUERBACH

2007–2011

Michigan Athletic Director Dave Brandon should have paid me to leave Ann Arbor.

I know it's more than a little absurd to blame me for what happened in Michigan athletics under my *Michigan Daily* tenure—since correlation is not causation and all that—but it's worth exploring my bad luck. I'm not sure a single *Daily* writer has had it worse.

As a sophomore, I covered the men's ice hockey team, a perennial CCHA power. The Wolverines I covered were fantastic at times during the regular season but limped into the postseason, winning neither their regular-season title nor the CCHA tournament. Still, they received a No. 1 seed in the NCAA tournament.

Three *Daily* writers and I drove through the night from Ann Arbor to bleary Bridgeport, Connecticut, for the tournament's first weekend. Less than 18 hours later, we were back on the road home, sleep-deprived but anxious to get away from a disastrous end to a season. Michigan had been shut out by Air Force, which had never before won an NCAA tournament game.

That two other No. 1 seeds went on to lose their opening-round games and the men's hockey tournament descended into chaos didn't really help. Michigan had been the best team in the nation for portions of the season, and the other writers and I truly thought we'd see it compete at the Frozen Four.

(Two seasons later, led by 5-foot-7 goaltender Shawn Hunwick,

135

Michigan made a most improbable run to the national championship game.)

Junior year, I moved on to covering the men's basketball team. Fresh off its first NCAA tournament appearance in 11 years, expectations were high. Ranked No. 15 in the preseason AP poll, a disjointed Michigan team stumbled to a 15–17 record by the end of the regular season, with three separate three-game losing streaks sprinkled in there. At the Big Ten Tournament, the Wolverines' season ended on a heartbreaking buzzer-beater from Evan Turner, a hated Buckeye. No NCAA tournament. No NIT. No postseason at all.

(Since that season, Michigan has gone dancing every year. Two years after Turner's shot, Michigan won a share of the Big Ten regular-season title for the first time in 26 years. One year after that, the Wolverines played for a national championship.)

My senior year came, and the football beat beckoned—the holy grail for a *Daily* sportswriter. I'd been around the football program a bit before (freelancing for the *Detroit Free Press* and SI.com) so I knew what I was getting into. My fellow beat writers and I would be documenting the make-or-break season for third-year coach Rich Rodriguez.

We covered the fallout from allegations of NCAA violations. We covered a historically bad defense—ranked 110th in the nation by season's end. We covered some thrilling moments—most notably, a 67–65 triple-overtime win against Illinois. And, of course, we covered the emergence of dual-threat quarterback Denard Robinson, who nearly single-handedly won that team a few games.

We watched Rodriguez's job security weaken after embarrassing, lopsided losses to Wisconsin and Ohio State. We watched a 52–14 loss to Mississippi State in the Gator Bowl, the proverbial nail in Rodriguez's coffin. I'll never forget what Rich Rod looked like walking through the stadium hallway to his Gator Bowl postgame press conference, his gaze on the ground, knowing he'd reached his end at Michigan.

I'll also never forget Rodriguez's final plea to Brandon, an athletic director who didn't hire him, and the divided Michigan fan base that never could quite figure out how to come together to support him. At the football team's annual banquet that year—which took place between the 30-point loss to Ohio State and the Gator Bowl—Rodriguez played Josh Groban's "You Raise Me Up," a song about overcoming troubles by receiving support from others. Rodriguez asked his wife, Rita, his players, and even Brandon all to hold hands while the lyrics rang out through the banquet hall.

(Four days after the Gator Bowl, Rodriguez was fired after posting a 15–22 record as Michigan's head coach. A week after that, Michigan announced the hire of Brady Hoke. In Hoke's first season, the Wolverines went 11–2 and won the Sugar Bowl.)

I used to hear stories from the *Daily* writers older than me, about their glory days, how so many of them got to cover national titles in various sports and Rose Bowl games. When I tried to explain my *Daily* experience to them, they acted as though I was speaking a foreign language. The teams I covered experienced more downs than ups, and more controversy than they'd have liked. But they were never boring.

They taught me something I've made sure to remember throughout my professional journalism career, too: Be a sportswriter because you like writing and telling stories, not because you like sports.

Sports are fickle. Team success fluctuates. Winning should never matter for someone who writes about sports for a living. Though we live in an age when it's become increasingly acceptable to write subjectively about sports (or at least wear your fandom proudly), I believe it's still important to keep your distance.

For me, it was easy to stay objective and write about Michigan sports that way, because I wasn't writing about winning all the time. I tried to find good stories to share, but I wasn't always writing about good things. In doing so, I learned how to be fair to the subjects of my stories, which has helped me in every single story I've written after leaving the *Daily*.

So maybe I didn't cover the best teams at Michigan, and maybe I missed out on NCAA tournament runs or unforgettable bowl games. But two years after I graduated, in my first season as a national college basketball writer for *USA Today*, the Michigan men's basketball team did make a run to the national championship game.

So, at the very least, I think the jinx is broken.

Nicole Auerbach covered a variety of sports for the *Michigan Daily* from 2007 to 2011, most notably men's ice hockey, men's basketball, and football. For her work covering the football team, she won the Big Ten's 2011 William R. Reed Award, an honor given to the Big Ten student journalist whose writing "best exemplifies the spirit, ideals, and dedication to the Big Ten and intercollegiate athletics." After graduating, she interned at the *Boston Globe* before landing a full-time job as a national college sports reporter at *USA Today*. She has held that position since September 2011.

PRESENT AT THE CREATION

ANDY KROLL

January 1–4, 2008

Mike Huckabee—former governor of Arkansas, Baptist minister, aw-shucks good ol' boy, and now Republican presidential contender—wants to introduce us to someone special, "a great American hero, ladies and gentleman, give a warm welcome to . . . *Chuck Norris!*" Several thousand people squeezed inside the Val Air Ballroom in West Des Moines go nuts. Walker Texas Ranger struts onstage in flannel and denim and gives a rousing plea to support Huck, a Man With Values, a God-fearing Christian who will get this country back on track. All we need to do is show up on Thursday and caucus for Mike Huckabee. Then Huckabee straps on his bass guitar and joins a local band called the Boogie Woogers in playing a chugging rendition of "Sweet Home Alabama" while Norris dances awkwardly stage right like a man with two sprained ankles.

The Val Air is an old-timey-themed place, and Huckabee's supporters shake and shimmy on the hard maple dance floor, farmers and homeschoolers and honest churchgoing folk from as far away as Florida. Think "Happy Days" meets the Moral Majority. And there I stand, a college reporter from the socialist enclave of Ann Arbor, Michigan, adrift in a sea of evangelicals. It's January 2, 2008. I am in Iowa covering the Democratic and Republican caucuses, the kick-off event in what would become one of the most historic presidential races in American history. It is my first real assignment as a reporter for the *Michigan Daily*, which happens to be my first job in journalism.

I watch Walker Texas Ranger sway to the sounds of the Boogie Woogers. Maybe I sway a little bit, too. I have been on the campaign trail for less than one hour.

In order to explain how I ended up in Iowa, you need to know how I landed at the *Daily*, which can get . . . complicated. By the time I arrived in Ann Arbor in the fall of 2007, my transcript listed four different institutions covering a three-year span: Marquette University, where I played college soccer and majored in women and beer; Oakland University, where I rode the bench and majored in weed; and then, after shelving my dreams of playing professional soccer, Kalamazoo Valley Community College and Western Michigan University, where I declared no major and had little idea what to do with my life. Call me a journeyman of higher education.

I had read a lot as a kid, plucking a volume or two off the walls of books I passed on my way to bed. The authors' names stared back at me: Jack London, Arthur Conan Doyle, Raymond Carver, Joan Didion. And I published the odd sports-themed opinion piece while still playing ball ("Why Coach Should Fly Coach" went the title of my rant about overpaid college coaches, which I thought was pretty clever at the time). There were practical concerns, too: My cozy one-bedroom on Packard wasn't going to pay for itself, and I'd prefer to get paid to create something rather than wiping down treadmills at the gym. So I turned up at 420 Maynard and climbed the steps to the *Daily* newsroom. The patter of typing, bantering sports editors, heaps of old marked-up copy, crumpled page proofs, yellowed editions of the *New York Times*, and bound volumes of the *Daily* opened to a story from years past: I had found a home I never knew existed.

The editor-in-chief was a hoodie-and-khakis-wearing Chicagoan named Karl Stampfl. Karl intimidated me: He was frighteningly talented, winning Hopwood writing awards like I won games of Halo. He calmly shredded our copy, circling sentences and boxing off whole paragraphs in red ink with a note: "SUCKS, MAKE BETTER." My first *Daily* byline attempted to reveal how the notoriously surly staff at a South Campus liquor store detected fake IDs. I ended up covering the doings of the Board of Regents and faculty senate with the zeal of David Halberstam, piling up enough clips that first semester to get promoted to news editor.

Then, a few days before the 2007 holiday break, an email lit up my inbox with the subject line: "Iowa?"

We were somewhere near the Iowa border when the terror hit. Our immediate problem: the blizzard engulfing our car, limiting visibility to a few dozen feet. All around us semis jackknifed and cars spun out and smacked into each other, straying off the road into five-foot-high snowdrifts. This is how my first real reporting assignment ends, I thought, stuck in a ditch waiting for AAA somewhere near a town called Peru, Illinois.

In truth, I couldn't decide what I feared more: Winding up marooned on the side of I-80 or actually making it to Iowa on time. The caucuses were the biggest political story since *Bush v. Gore*, a battle royal with enough drama and plot twists to fill a season of "Days of Our Lives." Clinton, Dodd, Edwards, Richardson, and Obama on the left; McCain, Romney, Giuliani, and Ron Paul on the right. A free-for-all, and reporters from all over the planet were descending on the Hawkeye State to cover it.

With me was a *Daily* photographer named Clif Reeder. He had his own problem: He had no gear. He'd left his professional cameras in Ann Arbor over the holiday break, and the blizzard had prevented me from returning to campus to retrieve them before picking up Clif in Chicago. In other words, we were a photographer without a camera and a reporter without a clue. The speedometer hovered around 40 miles per hour as we crawled across the heartland.

The blizzard whimpered just past the state line. Iowa was suicidally bleak in winter—flattened cornfields, spectral trees, and a slate-gray sky. We found the Days Inn on the outskirts of Des Moines that evening, swung by the Huckabee event at the Val Air, and then headed back to the room to crash. But before sensing a smell: Pot seeping out from under the door across the hall where some journalists on the digital team for a big TV network were staying. At least something in Iowa felt like home.

The next day, we drove to the Des Moines convention center to get our press passes and scope out the press filing room, the nerve center of the Political-Media-Industrial Complex. Step through a blue curtain and there they were, hundreds of journalists bent over their laptops, *tap-tap-tapping*, cellphones cradled between the shoulders and ears.

But the story, of course, was out there, in the VFW halls and high school gymnasiums, the diners and coffee shops and homes of real-life Iowans. Clif and I tore across the state in pursuit of the candidates with no shortage of events to attend. The challenge was choosing who to see without not spending half the day in the car crisscrossing the state. We settled into a routine: Arrive early, find the best spots for Clif to shoot from, and hunker down until the candidate arrives. Then, on the way back to the hotel, Clif drove while I furiously pounded out my story. So it went, four or five times a day, dusk to dark, black coffee, no cream no sugar, please and thank you.

Being a student journalist had its advantages on the trail. In the cutthroat world of campaign journalism, where the herd scraps and claws (and, if necessary, backstabs) for scoops and access, we got the cub treatment. I traded Emergen-C vitamin boosters for trade talk and job advice. Camera-less Clif befriended a gaggle of photographers at each campaign stop who freely shared a camera or a lens worth more than my student loans.

Looking back years later, much of the trip is a blur. But I remember one event like it was yesterday. We arrive hours early to an empty coffee shop near the University of Iowa in Iowa City. I bury my face in my laptop for a few hours, prewriting a few stories and typing up interview notes with "youth leaders" from around the state. I pick my head up occasionally to see a few more bodies trickle in, and like a time-lapse sequence, the coffee shop slowly begins to fill. At the appointed time, the candidate has not yet arrived, but people are standing on tables and lined up three-deep outside in the cold to steal a glimpse of him through the foggy windows. When the candidate finally arrives, he emerges from an employee-only door to a roar. Light fixtures rattle, windows shake. A small space opens up in the crowd just large enough for him to stand and speak. It gave me chills, the sight of so many young people drawn to this candidate and his vision of a united country, not a divided one. With his mega-watt smile and easy charm, I think, *This guy will be president.* John Edwards will be our next president.

We never saw Hillary Clinton—her events were overrun with reporters and TV trucks. She was still the presumptive Democratic candidate, and her campaign team swaggered around downtown Des Moines like they owned the place (and, for that matter, the country). This wasn't an election for them; it was a coronation.

Nor did we follow Obama too closely. His staffers were cool to us journalists—less interested in talking about the busloads of students pouring into Iowa to canvass for Obama than putting those busloads of students to work.

On the final night, we were watching a caucus take place in a high school auditorium in Des Moines when Clif's phone rang. An editor back in Ann Arbor was on the line.

"Just now? *Really?*"

Clif cupped the phone and looked at me. "CNN just called it for Obama."

Obama? The guy who'd run third in nearly every poll leading up to caucus night? We sprinted outside and jumped into the Taurus and squealed out of the parking lot headed downtown. By the time we reached the arena, it was crawling with press—every third rental car in the state of Iowa was parked outside. We ran into the arena and entered the scrum of journalists penned off to the side of the stage where Obama was to speak.

The crowd, squeezed together at the foot of the stage to give the appearance of a packed house for the TV cameras, went nuts just in time for the networks to go live to Obama's victory speech. And just like that, Obama was no longer the outsider, the rookie senator with the middle name Hussein. He was the frontrunner. The race was his to lose.

I don't remember a word of Obama's victory speech, and the video footage doesn't capture how it felt to be in that moment. I do remember seeing some of the biggest names in journalism: the *Washington Post*'s David Broder and the *New York Times* chief political correspondent Adam Nagourney, standing elbow to elbow with Maureen Dowd, the *Times* columnist, who used the same Steno pad that I did.

I felt like a minor leaguer who'd gotten called up to the bigs. I type that sentence and in my head I hear Karl Stampfl saying to me: "Sucks, make better." He's right, but on that cold night in Iowa, in some small way, I felt like I'd made it.

Andy Kroll was a reporter and news editor at the *Michigan Daily* from 2007 to 2009, a contributor to *The Statement* magazine and the paper's first investigative editor. Since graduating, he has worked as a staff writer in the San Francisco and Washington, D.C. bureaus of *Mother Jones*. He is now a magazine staff correspondent for *National Journal* covering the circus of American politics. He longs for Zingerman's smoked whitefish every single day.

WHO KNOWS BEST?

TIM ROHAN

October 2009 to March 2010

The first time I met Red Berenson, I was terrified. It was fall of my sophomore year, and the *Michigan Daily* had just placed me on the hockey beat. Now the four of us were gathered on the second-level terrace of Yost Ice Arena, overlooking the rink. Stone-faced and silent, the venerable coach reached out for a handshake.

I made sure to grip his hand firmly and look him in the eyes. Those piercing blue eyes. He looked me up and down, still silent. He could tell from my sweaty palms, I'm sure, that I knew nothing about hockey. Really, nothing. I thought the cycling involved bicycles, and I had no idea where the slot was. I had never watched a full game through, which is why I had never wanted to cover hockey in the first place.

Before I ever came to Michigan, I made a deal with my mother. I would major in engineering—as she had at Michigan—but only if I could spend my free time at the *Daily*. Growing up, I loved sports and dabbled in sports writing in high school at her suggestion. At Michigan, I sought out 420 Maynard before classes started. I wrote the requisite five articles to become an official *Daily* sportswriter in only about six weeks, which set a record. That's what I told my friends, anyway.

That fall, I was the only freshman picked to cover the women's basketball team, along with two sophomores, Joe Stapleton and Ryan Kartje. I was on the fast track. I started spending more time at the *Daily*, just hanging around. (At that age, almost anyone older than me seemed

143

cool.) The older writers started talking to me more, my writing slowly started to improve, and the *Daily* started to feel like home.

Then my father died.

Most of my life, he had suffered from Parkinson's disease. I wrote a eulogy and read it at his funeral, and as cliché as it sounds, I decided then that life is short, that I should do what I love. And I loved the *Daily*, the place, the people, so I further immersed myself, picking up extra stories, staying late, going on road trips.

The next year, when it came time for the senior editors to choose the basketball and hockey beats, Joe and I were living together in an apartment on State Street. We stayed up late, playing basketball on the courts outside of the Central Campus Recreation Building, going over scenarios, trying to count votes. The senior editors would interview candidates, including themselves, and decide. Following the typical progression, you would cover women's basketball, hockey, men's basketball, and then finally, football.

I wanted to cover men's basketball, to skip ahead. And the editors were my friends. I figured I would get what I wanted. No, I decided I *deserved* what I wanted.

Now I was shaking Berenson's hand for what seemed like forever.

Writers older than me were picked to cover basketball—seniority ruled. The editors, my friends, told me the hockey beat was the best training for a young writer. The season was unrelenting, from October to March, and you worked weekends, sure. But the access was incredible. You could attend almost any practice, interview whomever you wanted. No other newspaper regularly covered the team. And Berenson looked mean, but was kind at heart. I wanted to hear none of it.

Life isn't fair, my mother reminded me, I had to pay my dues. Pay my dues? The *Daily* was run by students. We were kids. But, I later learned, that's what made the place special. With no adults around, we developed egos, played monkey-in-the-middle on swivel chairs in the newsroom, and made mistakes. We had to learn from one another, trust one another. Trust that those older than us knew best.

I was mad, but I also didn't have much choice.

The others on the beat promised to teach me the sport. The hockey beat included Ryan, me, and two other sophomores, Mike Florek and Nick Spar. A part of me was jealous Mike and Nick had caught up. Mike had played hockey all his life, and Nick had played, too, and was the best writer among us. I feared falling behind.

For our season preview issue, while we were still getting to know each other, Nick, Mike, and I collaborated on a feature on the defensemen. We decided to each write a section and paste them together at the end: The other two would write about the actual strategy, and I would write about the group bonding over some superstition about athletic tape. We brought it in the night the section went to print, and the final draft was unrecognizable—red ink covered each section, as if the pen had leaked.

We were all humbled a bit by that, I think, and soon we became close friends, stopping for Colliders at Rod's Diner, going to house parties on Friday nights.

Nick and I later ran the sports section together, and now, years after graduating, I still send him my rough drafts to edit. He actually left the beat that winter for a five-month internship with the White House. (Yes, he was the best among us.)

By the time Nick left, I had stopped sulking. I attended practice four days a week, sat in the stands, and picked Mike's brain. Most days, I spent much of the time trying to figure out who was who and who was on which line. My favorite part was the shootouts at the end of practice, hockey in its simplest form. That, I understood.

Afterward, we interviewed players as they came off the ice, and eventually I developed a routine, asking general questions first to get them talking, and then relying on follow-up questions to figure out what was interesting or important. Were my questions dumb? Probably. (My beatmates once almost convinced me to ask about a fictitious hockey play they said was called "The Phantom.") But then I took what I learned from the players into our interviews upstairs with Red.

At some point, he had become simply "Red." We always interviewed him in the same lounging area outside the locker room, where he always sat in the same spot, at the end of a leather couch, clutching a coffee cup, and always answered our questions calmly, in a way I could understand. Most every week, Mike and I went to his radio show to hear someone else ask him questions, because he could be stubborn.

His aura demanded a certain level and balance of respect and fear. He had starred at Michigan, played 17 years in the NHL, became a coach, and won the NHL Coach of the Year in 1981. A few years later, he returned to coach and resurrect his struggling alma mater. Now 30 years later, he has two national titles; has more than 800 wins—the fourth most in college hockey history; and, at one point, led Michigan to a record 22 consecutive NCAA tournament appearances. The Streak, we called it.

Red was a living legend, the Bo of Michigan hockey.

He turned 70 that December and still kept up with the teenagers at practice. He told us stories about his childhood in Saskatchewan, Canada, the time he scored six goals in a game, and how pucks were made. Getting him to open up was a *Daily* rite of passage.

He respected us, I think, mostly because we cared and we tried. Before the season, Mike and I had made a pact to have a writer at every game, no matter the distance. I went to Alaska by myself (Thanks, Mom.); spent Halloween weekend in Sault Ste. Marie with Mike; felt Camp Randall Stadium shake as Michigan played Wisconsin outdoors; drove through the night, in a snowstorm, to get to Omaha. On the car rides, we talked nonstop about the team. No one knew it better than us.

Toward the end of the season, a clear, defining storyline emerged.

On senior night at Yost, the starting goalie, Bryan Hogan, injured his groin and was replaced by Shawn Hunwick, the walk-on backup who stood 5-feet, 7-inches and was the younger brother of Matt Hunwick, a former Michigan hockey star.

At the time, Michigan was in serious danger of missing the NCAA tournament. The team had underachieved all season, which had clearly caused Red some frustration. About a week later, Michigan entered its conference tournament as the No. 7 seed, likely needing to win it to earn an automatic NCAA berth and extend The Streak.

With Hunwick in net, Michigan stormed through the tournament, beating three of the conference's top four teams—Michigan State, Miami (Ohio), and Northern Michigan. Hunwick was named tournament MVP. It all felt like something out of the movie *Rudy*, if Rudy had almost single-handedly saved his team's season.

Michigan eventually lost to Miami (Ohio) 3–2 in double overtime in the NCAA Midwest Regional Final in Fort Wayne, Indiana—one goal away from the Frozen Four. It was an epic game, ripe with emotion, which made my game story so easy to write. The beat I never wanted taught me sports writing was first and foremost about storytelling, no matter the sport. That's what I had done all year. *That's* what I loved.

That night, us *Daily* writers were the last ones to leave the arena. We lingered for a few minutes, reminiscing. It was *Daily* sports tradition to steal something on road trips, so as we left, Mike and I took the plush blue folding chairs we were sitting on as souvenirs.

The hockey beat had been worth commemorating, after all.

Tim Rohan worked as a *Michigan Daily* sportswriter from 2008 to 2012 and served as co-managing sports editor in 2011. After graduation, he worked as the *New York Times* summer sports intern and, on one of his first assignments, happened to cover the first no-hitter in Mets' history. His internship was subsequently extended through the end of the year, during which he served as the *Times* national college football writer. Afterward, over the next four months, he freelanced for the *Times* and happened to be covering the 2013 Boston Marathon. In the aftermath, he spent three months reporting and writing a feature story on a victim, Jeff Bauman, titled "Beyond the Finish Line." The *Times* hired him as an intermediate reporter soon after and nominated his marathon story for a Pulitzer Prize in feature writing. *Sports Illustrated* also named him to its 2013 Top 25 Under 25 list. He currently works in the *Times* sports department covering the Mets.

CUT TO MICHIGAN

ANDREW LAPIN

2010–2011

When you're a film buff at a school known more for its Big House than any big screens, you need to have a support group. That's how I came to be a member of the *Michigan Daily* Film Squad, the small band of arts writers who had come together over our shared love of arguing about movies. We were a special bunch, full of fiery passion for the Coen brothers and Hayao Miyazaki, yet we were the most useless members of the *Daily*'s writing staff.

We reviewed every film that opened within Ann Arbor's city limits, cramming the arts section with dissertations on children's movies and gross-out comedies instead of content with any specific University angle. Our mission to emulate Roger Ebert was met with consternation from the managing editor, who quietly stomached our obsession with the good, bad, and ugly of the medium, and indifference at best from readers, who would check Rotten Tomatoes if they really wanted someone's opinion on a movie.

But thanks to Michigan's government, the national film scene did become a local issue. In 2008, the year I joined the *Daily*, Governor Jennifer Granholm signed a law granting filmmakers in the Great Lakes state tax rebates worth up to 42 percent of their production costs, with no cap. The insanely generous offer made Michigan the friendliest state in America to movie producers. With these incentives in place, suddenly there was reason for students to care about the movies: celebrities. My peers swarmed the Michigan League for the chance to be extras in George

Clooney's political thriller *The Ides Of March*; surreptitiously snapped photos of Clive Owen and David Schwimmer outside the undergraduate library shooting their Internet-predator drama *Trust*; and swapped tales of what Pierce Brosnan, in town to play a faith healer in the religious satire *Salvation Boulevard*, had ordered at The Chop House on Main Street.

Myself, I had a conversation with Jason Segel on the corner of State and North University streets, when he was filming *The Five-Year Engagement*, a comedy about a couple who move to Ann Arbor and promptly become miserable. It went like this:

ME: Hey, are you Jason Segel?
JASON: Yeah, man. How's it going?
ME: Great!

This was all fun, and made for some killer stories to trade at Film Squad meetings while we avoided assigning real stories. But the responsible arts editor in me knew the real newsy benefit to the film tax incentives was the enormous economic boost they would give Michigan's film production industry, and by extension, University students desperate to prove they didn't need to go to school in New York or Los Angeles to get a foothold in the movies. I was willingly seduced by the possibility of a real, honest-to-God cinema movement in the Mitten State. So when I was *Daily* editor-in-chief in the summer of 2010, I set aside part of the editorial travel budget to follow a group of Screen Arts and Cultures students to the Traverse City Film Festival where they premiered their class movies.

While in Traverse City I grew friendly with my sources. I wasn't in their program, but I took every elective I could in the department, and the knowledge I most readily absorbed dealt with film theory. These SAC students were my people. They joked about framing each other in impeccable shots, traded frustrations about their screenplays' fatal flaws, whiled away afternoons watching rare Region 2 Japanese DVDs in the University's Donald Hall Collection. I spent hours talking to them about films, about the strange, magical power they held, and about how wonderful it would be to make movies in Michigan for a living.

And so I did what no journalist should ever do: I rooted for my sources. I clapped loudly when they screened their films at the festival. And I kept clapping afterward, when dozens of them clambered up on stage one by one to accept levels of audience gratitude that my friends in the English department, weaned on polite claps at thesis readings, would have found excessive. (Such sustained congratulations for a few months of work on a short student film? No wonder everyone in Hollywood has big egos; they need to fit in all those claps.) I returned to Ann Arbor from the festival hoping the incentives program would succeed.

Later that summer I visited the set of the first film from the Michigan Creative Film Alliance, a joint effort between the University of Michigan, Michigan State University, and Wayne State University to make a collaborative student film that could demonstrate the raw talent at the state's three biggest research schools. The universities divided every task on set, so a Spartan cameraman took instructions from the Wolverine director, while a Warrior applied makeup, and so on. The program's inaugural movie was *Appleville*, a comic thriller about two guys who attempt to rob a nursing home charter bus to pay for a medical procedure. Faculty advisors likened it to "*Speed* on a senior citizens' bus." It didn't make a lot of sense, but these were my peers, so I was willing to suspend my disbelief.

And I had a blast spending the day just out of frame. At one point it stormed, big fat raindrops plopping on an exterior set with expensive equipment, and I watched the all-student crew scamper every which way in their desperate attempt to salvage the production. I reveled in the chaos, because I knew it would breed a flesh-and-blood *movie*, that thing we in Film Squad lived to treasure. I was more proud of the feature story I produced from these outings than anything else I wrote at the *Daily*.

As Rick Snyder ascended to the governor's office in 2011, hinting that our generous incentives would be on the chopping block, the cries and protests began to swell:

Save our movies.

Keep our best talent in Michigan.

Yet Snyder did as many suspected, and laid out his proposal in March 2011 to sharply reduce the incentive program. That same month, I attended the *Appleville* premiere at the Detroit Film Theatre, which now served a larger purpose as a rally to preserve Michigan's movie money. The red carpet, the gorgeous palatial venue, the never-ending introductions from professors and state film office advisory council: All of it was in service of this greater cause. Sitting in the front row, even as I began to fidget from the bloat of the presentation, I felt a note of pride that, through my articles, I had helped bring attention to the issue in some small way. Then the movie started.

Immediately, the Film Squadder in me—the guy who loves to dissect the art of the craft, the guy who fell in love with movies in the first place— knew that what was unspooling in the Detroit Film Theatre was an utter mess. Characters ran around with murderous intentions and paper-thin motives. Sound effects looped incessantly and didn't match what was happening onscreen. There were technical errors all over the place, and the editing style was so slapdash the movie was nearly incoherent. In their effort to compress a feature-length script into a 25-minute short, the *Appleville* team had evoked *Speed* in only the worst way: The film couldn't slow down, even when it would have been a good idea.

In short, *Appleville* was not the best way to alert Michigan to the bright young filmmaking talent at risk of leaving the state. But the Michigan Creative Film Alliance had at least preserved one Hollywood element: the gaudy back-patting of a movie premiere in outsized proportion to the amount of work that preceded it. Everyone from the line producer to the sound mixers to the extras who played the senior citizens gave speeches praising the students' professionalism, their gifted work ethic, the success they were poised for if only the state would let them.

As I squirmed in my seat throughout the 25-minute film and the 40 minutes of self-congratulation that followed, another, more terrifying thought occurred to me: What if these *were* Michigan's best and brightest young filmmakers? What if this patchwork jumble of sounds and images truly was the best we could offer to the industry? If some big shot from Hollywood had only this movie to go on, there'd be no second chance— they'd simply deem us unworthy of attention, and move on.

I realized my feature on *Appleville* had betrayed the basic Film Squad ethos: The backstory behind a movie was always secondary to the fundamental question of whether it was any good. The short film stood for economic opportunity, but economic opportunity doesn't count for much to the audience.

The tax benefits didn't completely vanish, but Snyder removed Granholm's unlimited tax rebate and replaced it with an overall cap of $25 million annually (at the time of publication, it had climbed to $50 million). The mood among the state's creatives was still funereal; the rug had been pulled out from under us, the promise of a robust homegrown movie machine up in flames. A converted studio in Pontiac where director

Sam Raimi, a Michigander, had filmed *Oz the Great and Powerful* was going unused, missing bond payments, and defaulting on loans.

"Our school's budding actors and filmmakers may be gone for good," wrote my friend and fellow Film Squad member, Kavi Shekhar Pandey, in a 2011 article for *The Statement*, the *Daily's* weekly magazine. All the University film students would flee to the Southern California Promised Land, burned once more by their state's fickle government spending decisions—like they had been in 2009 when the legislature ended the Michigan Promise college scholarships midway through parceling them out to eligible in-state students. Another promise broken. Who can blame them for leaving?

Four years later, there's certainly less overall film-related work in the state, but the incentive reduction hasn't been as apocalyptic as its detractors had feared—at least, not when it comes to celebrity sightings. The state has continued to land big-spending blockbusters, from the fourth *Transformers* movie to *Batman v Superman: Dawn of Justice,* the latter of which was Michigan's biggest-scale production to date when it filmed in Pontiac and Detroit in 2014. Stars like Mark Wahlberg, Ben Affleck, and Ryan Gosling have continued to bless Detroit and its surrounding cities with their presence.

In another time, Film Squad might have eagerly awaited the opportunity to mock the quality of these made-in-Michigan movies, but we have some distance from the excitement now. Our members are dispersed across the country: a schoolteacher in West Bloomfield, a political strategist in Washington, D.C., a producer in Hollywood (someone finally made it to the other side of the screen). We no longer congregate every Sunday to hotly debate Quentin Tarantino's oeuvre while not turning in content for the paper.

I, however, have continued on my foolhardy quest to write about movies for a living, a quest that the *Daily* and my Film Squad editors (perhaps erroneously) taught me was something to strive for. For a brief, shining moment, Rotten Tomatoes even designated me as a Top Critic, with the star and everything. And I'm still an unapologetic homer for any movie that has some connection to Michigan. When I reviewed *The Five-Year Engagement* for NPR, I gave it a glowing recommendation, despite the fact that by the end of that film, Jason Segel can't wait to get the hell out of Ann Arbor.

I also keep in touch with Michigan friends in Hollywood. Recently, one noted, "In like 30 years when we are producing movies, Andrew Lapin is going to be a famous film critic and he is going to shit on our lives." I grinned at the sentiment, but that's never been my intention. I remember how annoyed I felt as a former Michigan Marching Band member when I walked into the *Daily* one fall Monday and the editor-in-chief was mocking the previous weekend's halftime show. It sucks when something you've worked on becomes someone else's target for snark. But there's a gulf between snark and blind, endless applause, and that gulf is filled with honesty. And the freedom to be honest—about art, and by extension, about life—was always what I truly loved about film criticism, even more than the movies themselves.

The Michigan Creative Film Alliance lasted another two years as a collaborative moviemaking endeavor; since premiering the short comedy *Downriver* in 2013, the group shifted its goals to serve as a general advocate for keeping movies in Michigan. And their films got better, so I've been told. I really do hope the state hosts a thriving film industry again, and I hope the *Daily* covers it, so long as that coverage is honest about the quality of the movies themselves. It's what Film Squad would have wanted.

Andrew Lapin joined the *Michigan Daily* in 2008 as a film writer and was a senior arts editor in 2010 and the summer editor-in-chief in 2010. While at the University of Michigan he also played trombone in the Michigan Marching Band and won a Hopwood Award for short fiction. After graduation he interned at NPR, was an editorial fellow at *Government Executive* magazine, and covered public media as an assistant editor for the trade paper *Current*. He is now a freelance journalist and film critic, and his film reviews and features have appeared in outlets, including NPR, the *Washington Post*, the *Atlantic*, the *Dissolve*, *Tablet*, and *Washington City Paper*. He was a fellow at the 2014 Tent Writers' Conference and a member of the 2014 Young Critics Workshop at Film Fest Gent in Belgium.

EXPECTING THE NEXT GREAT SOCIETY

JILLIAN BERMAN

May 1, 2010

To say I have an affinity for Lyndon B. Johnson is an understatement. There are two pictures of him in my bedroom. I'm currently plowing my way through Robert Caro's voluminous biography of the man my favorite high school history teacher described as "the most tragic president," remembered for escalating the Vietnam War instead of for his "Great Society"—an ambitious anti-poverty agenda he proposed at none other than Michigan Stadium.

So when the University announced President Barack Obama would deliver the commencement address in 2010, I was hoping for another Great Society moment. One of the things that always appealed to me about being a reporter is the opportunity to write the first draft of history. I thought this would be my chance to really do that.

When Obama was elected in 2008, I ran out to the Diag with almost everyone in the newsroom to cover students' reactions. But eager as I was to interview excited students and jot down notes about the hundreds of students chanting, banging on drums, and celebrating, as a sophomore low on the *Daily*'s totem pole, I knew little of what I collected would end up in the main story.

Fast-forward two years, and I was one of the paper's top editors. "This is my historical moment," I thought of Obama's commencement address. I interviewed experts about what the president might say, and they confirmed my inklings.

Presidents don't just come to Michigan—one of the biggest public universities in the nation, in the backdrop of the most famous blue-collar industry—for nothing. They come to announce something big. As any good Michigan student knows, John F. Kennedy launched the Peace Corps from the steps of the Michigan Union. Gerald Ford announced his re-election campaign at the University. And of course, there was Johnson's Great Society.

Sitting in the pen on the field at the Big House anticipating Obama with professional reporters and two of my closest *Daily* friends, my skin was tingling. I had goosebumps. I was prepared to cry inappropriately. But Obama's speech was, frankly, a dud. He took the opportunity to make a political statement, decrying the partisan rhetoric he was so often on the wrong end of. No major policy programs, not even a nod at boosting all American students so they could end up at a place like Michigan.

The history nerd and progressive in me felt cheated. But I had a job to do. As the ceremony ended, I wandered out of the stadium, tracking down excited students in caps and gowns to ask them what they thought. What I found is they were largely disappointed too.

My account of their "meh" reactions to the president's speech was the first story I ever had published on The Huffington Post, where I worked after graduation. The site's college editors played it prominently, dedicating just a small headline to a story on what Obama actually said. Obviously, I was pleased to have my piece carried on a national site, but it also helped me re-evaluate how best to document what's happening now for those in the future. Most of the time, the real story isn't what the important people say and do—after all you can get that information from a variety of sources, including the records of the power players themselves—it's how those things affect everyone else.

I only came to this conclusion shortly after the last story I ever wrote for the *Daily* published, but looking back, I now realize that was the type of journalism I was learning to do all along. Most of the reporting I did at the *Daily* wasn't intense document probes or covering administrators' speeches. Instead, I was the queen of the dreaded "man on the street" interview. I heard students' opinions on everything from undocumented immigrants to the closing of a beloved NYPD Pizza location, and in the process, soaked up whatever I could about the diverse opinions on campus.

My favorite conversations, though, were with my colleagues at the *Daily*. In between NFL playoff banter and fights over Kanye West, we talked seriously about how we should play stories and the best angles to pursue—ultimately developing the paper's viewpoint. Yes, we tried to cover everything fairly and without bias, but the *Daily* has never been shy about being an advocate for students by reporting the news from their perspective.

Nowhere was this more evident than in the special edition we produced to hand out at that disappointing commencement. The stories in there showcased our highest hopes for the president's speech. Even though Obama didn't live up to those expectations, his face still occupies a place on my wall next to Lyndon Johnson.

He's gazing out over Michigan Stadium, an image *Daily* designers created for the cover of that lofty handout. Every time I look at it, I'm reminded of that rainy graduation day and how it was there that I finally realized the kind of stories I want to tell.

Jillian Berman began working at the *Michigan Daily* in 2007. She covered the campus life beat and was the paper's managing news editor in 2010. Her work has appeared in Bloomberg and *USA Today*. After graduation, she was a reporter for The Huffington Post's business section, where she covered retail, the food industry, and gender politics in the workplace. She's currently a reporter at MarketWatch, where she covers student debt and financial issues facing young people.

CHASING AFTER SHOELACE

RYAN KARTJE

November 2010

There's a collage that hangs directly above my desk in one corner of my one bedroom apartment in Santa Monica, where I've lived for the past two years. It's a compilation of some of the most important articles of my very young journalism career, kindly and lovingly made for me by my mom. She gave it to me as a birthday present three years ago. I've looked at it almost every day since.

The collage has come to mean a lot of different things to me in those three years. It's been a reminder of my amazing days at the *Michigan Daily* or at my internship with *USA Today*. It's a sign of how lucky I was to do what I did with my time in Ann Arbor. But mostly, it's a trigger for one of my greatest fears as a budding writer—that, one day, I might peak.

"They Call Him Shoelace" holds a prominent place in the collage. It's still one of the best stories I've ever written, and ever since it printed, I've been chasing the same sort of high. All three jobs I've held since graduating from the University of Michigan were made possible because of "They Call Him Shoelace." It published on November 4, 2010. That's over four years ago now.

I've learned since then that stories like that are lucky and fleeting and only come around every once in a while. It takes everything in you as a journalist to find them and grab on. That certainly was the case with "They Call Him Shoelace," when, for days, I skipped class and sat in a dark room on East Jefferson Street in Ann Arbor in boxer shorts and a white T-shirt and refused to come out until I'd crafted a masterpiece.

I can't believe they let me go.

That's all I could think as my plane took off from Detroit Metro, on its way to Fort Lauderdale, where my biggest story waited patiently for me just a few miles north in the muggy Florida town of Deerfield Beach. Of course, I had no idea. But now, one national first place award and three jobs later—all of which were made possible because of this story—I'd be lying if I said it wasn't blind luck that got me to Deerfield.

Before my senior year and second semester as managing sports editor of the *Michigan Daily*, I met with the three other members of the *Daily*'s football beat at Espresso Royale on State Street. We sipped coffee at a corner table, throwing around story ideas, and I had one that I felt particularly connected to.

Denard Robinson, a dynamic dual threat quarterback from Florida, was poised to push Tate Forcier for Michigan's starting job, and something about Robinson drew me in. He had this aura I couldn't quite explain. He was always smiling, always happy, and his speed was unlike anything I'd seen for a college quarterback. And, as you know if you've ever heard of Denard, he played with his shoelaces untied.

So I called dibs. If Denard Robinson were to become newsworthy, I wanted to be the one to write his story. It seems incendiary now. But I assure you: It was no more than dumb luck.

From there, Robinson proceeded to captivate the nation with one of the best seasons for a running quarterback in the history of college football. For six-straight weeks, he ran for at least 100 yards and a touchdown. He shot up Heisman Trophy candidate lists. Around campus, he was already on his way to becoming a legend—a bright spot in a dark era for Michigan football. The story grew exponentially. Each week, my eyes widened.

And soon, my story was in motion. I asked the Athletic Department for a one-on-one interview with Denard a few weeks into the season and was denied. With each huge performance, I asked again, and every week, I got the same answer.

I came to our editor-in-chief, Jake Smilovitz, with an idea. What if I went to Denard's hometown? What if I didn't bother interviewing him at all?

I'd set up just two interviews—a loosely planned meeting with Denard's peewee coach and a post-game interview with his high school coach—and I'd heard a rumor that his family gathered to watch every Michigan football game at a tailgate somewhere in Deerfield Beach. Honestly, I had no idea what might happen. It was not exactly an inspiring story pitch.

The trip was also going to cost upwards of $1,500, and there was still a potential bowl game the sports section had to save up for. I assumed I'd get another no and that the story would fade away.

But Jake said yes.

So there I was, set to land in Fort Lauderdale with *Daily* photographer Max Collins, two interviews, and a few unanswered voicemails left at numbers I heard, secondhand, might be connected to the Robinson family. It wasn't long before the panic and the self-doubt set in.

As the sports editor at the time, I'd tried to carve out a niche for myself as a feature writer. I loved (and still love) long, winding narratives. It was part of my campaign when I ran for sports editor—to spread the gospel of longform to as many *Daily* writers as I could.

So the pressure to perform in this particular instance was especially heavy. Before I left, the message was clear: Make this worth it.

I thought about that a lot during my first day walking around Deerfield Beach, as the humid Florida sun weighed heavy on the landscape.

It wasn't until my third day that I got my lucky break.

It came in a parking lot of a local park, tucked right next to the city's projects. A few blocks away, kids stood on a street corner selling drugs. It struck me then how easily Denard could have been forgotten in this town, mixed up in this or that, selling drugs, or running with a gang.

For weeks, I tried to locate Denard's family, but so far, they had eluded me, clearly nervous to talk to a reporter. But almost on accident, during one of the two interviews I had set up before leaving Michigan, Sammie Huggins had finally opened the door.

Years ago, Huggins was Denard's peewee coach—a rotund man, who sported a clunky gold chain around his neck and spoke in a deep, joyful voice. Denard's family, he said, was sitting around a television in his grandmother's driveway as we spoke, preparing to watch Michigan take on Iowa. He called Dorothea, Denard's mother, to ask if it was alright to bring us over. After some convincing, she complied. To this day, I'm not exactly sure why she felt compelled to say yes.

An hour later, I sat in a white lawn chair under a tent in Rose Robinson's driveway, eating potato salad and drinking grape soda. I scrambled down notes on everything I saw and heard, having decided on the flight over that I would use my recorder as little as possible. At the party—which would eventually be the primary scene for my story—it made all the difference.

Denard's aunts and uncles were full of life, asking me questions and

Photo by Max Collins

telling me their stories. But it was Denard's parents who drew me in. Both were leery of Max and me. Neither had much to say. Neither took their eyes off the screen for long.

It was the third quarter when Denard went down and didn't get up. He injured his shoulder and wouldn't return to play that game. A wave of dread and anxiety washed over the entire tailgate, and for a moment, I was sure all the story angles that had come about from my experience in this makeshift driveway amphitheatre might be ruined.

Then, as the game neared its end, Dorothea and Thomas, Denard's father, finally came together at the front of the tailgate. It was the first time I'd see them together all day. Dorothea's hands were on Thomas' shoulders, and for a fleeting moment, I could see exactly what the story was about.

It was a beautifully real moment, a mother and a father watching a small television, worried about their son, who, to everyone else, was just an injury-prone quarterback. They said almost nothing to each other, but they didn't need to.

I'd spent several days in Deerfield Beach by that point and talked to as many people as I could about Denard. I interviewed teachers and coaches at Deerfield Beach High. I ate spicy wings and drank beer with his high school football coach. I searched high and low for clues to what and who made Denard who he was. But nothing compared to this moment, watching the two people who loved him the most, the two people who helped shape him, who had gotten him out of Deerfield Beach, where most kids like Denard rarely leave. Their eyes said everything.

This was the story, the fleeting moment I came more than 1,300 miles for.

Of course, I'd be lying if I said it was that easy.

I wrote the entire plane ride home. It was mostly dribble. The first (very) rough draft barely gave the tailgate any justice. When I landed, I deleted at least half of what I'd written out of frustration.

That Sunday, the *Daily*'s sports section gathered for our weekly meeting. Each week at these gatherings, John Lowe, the Tigers beat writer for the *Detroit Free Press*, gave a lecture on journalism—invaluable information for someone who wants to actually be a sportswriter.

When John gave his week's lesson, I was distracted, agonizing over the story. He told the room to email the writers they admired and to try and contact as many great writers as they could. I tuned out most of the lecture, but for some reason, that particular bit of advice struck a chord with me. As soon as I got home, I emailed Wright Thompson, a longform writer for ESPN.com. He called me two hours later.

Without Wright, the story wouldn't have been what it is today. His first advice was to delete what I'd already written. The tailgate, he said, was where the magic was. That moment between his mother and father, the love of a family watching their son—that was the story.

From Monday to Wednesday I then wrote and wrote for hours straight. I skipped class. I ate way too much pizza. I learned more about sports writing in those three days than I had in the past year.

As I looked at the final draft, marked up with final edits from Wright, I was sleep deprived and had briefly forgotten what the sun looked like. But it was one of the more satisfying moments of my life. I brought it to Jake that night and watched him as he sat at his desk, reading with a red marker in his hand. After he read the story, he hugged me.

To this day, I'm not sure I could tell you the formula for writing a perfect story. I'm not sure I could even get you halfway there. I'm still chasing that enlightenment, like any other writer worth his or her salt.

All the time, I think about Denard and the dumb luck and chance opportunities and amazing people it took to write something that, at the time, felt like the best story I could possibly write. But I've realized in these few years that pushing forward, past your own ceiling, is the only way a writer can really continue climbing.

Photo by Max Collins.

The picture in the collage near my desk is of Denard's father at the tailgate, looking on anxiously at an image of his son on the television.

It's a beautiful picture, by any measure, and it's bursting with meaning. But as I've gotten older and realized how truly far I have to go as a writer, it's become a symbol of those fleeting, subtly powerful moments that jumpstarted my career, the moments I hope to spend my life chasing.

Ryan Kartje worked as a *Michigan Daily* sportswriter from 2008 to 2011, serving as managing sports editor during his final year at the paper. During his tenure at the *Daily*, he won the Society of Professional Journalists Sports Story of the Year award for his piece, "They Call Him Shoelace," on Michigan quarterback Denard Robinson. After interning with *USA Today* following graduation, he bounced around from the *Bloomington (Ind.) Herald Times*, where he won an Associated Press Sports Editors award for his coverage of Hoosiers basketball, to FoxSportsWisconsin.com, where he covered the Milwaukee Brewers and Bucks. Now, after having three jobs in three years, he finds himself on the West Coast, where he has written for the *Orange County Register* since November 2012. He currently covers University of California–Los Angeles sports and resides in Santa Monica, California.

CLOSE UP

CHANTEL JENNINGS

March 20, 2011

Of course we left on Saint Patrick's Day.

The *Michigan Daily* always had a way of trumping any social event I had planned with friends, so my coverage of the Michigan basketball team playing in the 2011 NCAA Tournament in Charlotte, North Carolina, would be no different.

The night before we left, I had endured one of my final senior editor shifts, trudging home from the newsroom sometime around 2:30 a.m. Two hours later my friends would wake me up for the annual St. Patrick's Day green eggs and ham party at a friend's house before heading to the bars at 6 a.m. This was, after all, what second semester senior year was supposed to be like.

Little sleep, Good Time Charley's bar, and last-minute packing is a basic summation of many memories for many *Daily* sportswriters.

A fellow basketball beat writer picked me up on Sybil Street early that afternoon. We would be pulled over by the cops (twice)—which only seemed right as it *was* a *Daily* sports road trip—on our 618 miles to Charlotte.

That night when we arrived one of my college roommates texted me, "Drinks later?"

I responded that I couldn't because I was in North Carolina. I sometimes told them when I was leaving to cover games. Other times it just slipped my mind. As if, "Hey, I'll be in North Carolina for either a day or maybe three, I don't know yet," were something the typical student had to consider.

But by this time, it was standard. I missed birthdays and festivities and whatever else college students celebrate (Cinco de Mayo, Cinco de Month-O, etc.) because I was in Evanston or Madison or Bloomington or Minneapolis.

When I had left for Charlotte, I still wasn't 100 percent sure I wanted to be in journalism or if it were worth everything I was missing. My friends were enjoying their final semester of college, while I was spending mine working 40 hours a week at a paper, choosing dress suits over short dresses for my weekend attire.

I thought my uncertainty meant I might be in the wrong field.

There was always that doubt because, according to people far smarter than me (my parents, professors, writers) journalism was an unstable field, and my English and Spanish majors could be used in so many different (read: better, as in monetarily better) ways. In fact, for my 21st birthday my parents gave me a book entitled "I'm An English Major—Now What?" Inscribed: "Love you! Mom and Dad."

I enjoyed journalism, and most days that feeling tide me over. But on my last St. Patrick's Day of college, I wondered if I would eventually regret how much time I had spent at the *Daily*.

We arrived in Charlotte that night—four college students snugly fit into one double room at a hotel that was actually nice, as opposed to the usual motel 20 miles outside of the city that may not have had a door lock, management, clean sheets, or all of the above. I thanked whichever *Daily* expense God finagled this one and quickly fell asleep.

That Friday the Michigan basketball team played at 12:40 p.m. in Time Warner Cable Arena against Bruce Pearl and Tennessee. Michigan would win. It would be Pearl's final game as a coach until he was hired by Auburn in 2014. I understood how the Volunteer fan base felt after that kind of disappointment. My years at Michigan could aptly be described as the four most unimpressive years in Michigan athletic history. My first football game as a student? Appalachian State. My last? Mississippi State.

But this Michigan basketball team had become one that I enjoyed watching. I grew up playing and studying the game, and I began coaching junior high teams when I finished playing. I loved transition offense and steals and improvisation. Now, this team was doing the same.

Following the game, my two fellow beat writers and the photographer informed me they would be heading back to Ann Arbor. They hadn't expected Michigan to win that day (honestly, neither had I), but they needed to return to campus.

Yes, Michigan would play that Sunday against No. 3 Duke, but they had to study. Or something like that.

Yes, our fourth beat writer would drive down the next day so I wouldn't be alone in covering the game. And they'd try to find a photographer to accompany him as well.

Yes, the Michigan Athletic Director offered to write them notes to get them extensions on their exams or papers so they could cover the event. But they were having none of it.

I was livid. It was the third round of the NCAA Tournament. It was Duke. It was Mike Krzyzewski and Kyrie Irving. It was the biggest event any of us had ever covered. A trip to the Sweet 16 was on the line.

And they were treating it like some intramural game.

Maybe two years or two months before I wouldn't have been angry, maybe I would've understood they wanted to take their academics seriously, maybe I wouldn't have taken it personally.

But I did.

In that moment I realized *my* classroom and *my* education was happening more in arenas and press conferences than in some Gothic hall on State Street. I didn't need a professor right then. I needed coaches and players. I needed a deadline column. I needed this game.

Something had changed. Maybe I didn't feel it on the car ride down or when I got that text from friends the night before, but standing in that arena, I knew I would've skipped anything to cover Michigan vs. Duke. And I couldn't understand someone—especially a writer—who didn't feel the same way.

So they left.

I stayed.

The next morning I got a phone call from the *Daily*'s managing photo editor who informed me she didn't have a single photographer who could make the trip to Charlotte to shoot the game. The fact that I expected a college student to make a last-minute, overnight trip to Charlotte, North Carolina, says a lot about the *Daily* and its newsroom.

"That's fine," I told her. "Send a camera. I'll do it."

She laughed.

"No, seriously," I said. "I'll do it."

The *Daily* hated using AP wire photos when we could get shots ourselves, and while I had never gone through any photography training or so much as held a *Daily* camera, she obligingly sent it.

She emailed a cheat sheet explaining aperture and ISO and shutter speed. A few other photographers at the arena tried to help me until they realized I didn't even know whether I'd be shooting with a Canon or Nikon. I was way past the college newspaper stigma and venturing into middle school journalism club territory (which, of course, I had never joined).

That night, my fellow beat writer arrived with the camera. (It was a Nikon.) I took it out of the case and tried snapping some photos in the hotel lobby. Terrible. I went outside to see if it was the lighting. Still terrible. I moved a few of the buttons. Nothing helped.

I was walking into a suicide mission, and I knew it. So naturally, I joined the *Detroit Free Press*, *Detroit News*, and national writers at a bar.

The next morning I walked to the stadium, computer bag over one shoulder, camera bag over the other. I found my seat on press row, set up my computer, gave one last call to the photo editor for good luck, and went to find the *Daily*'s assigned photo seat on the baseline.

Apparently, photographers bring little chairs and cushions with them to shoot games. I didn't know this. Apparently, they also don't wear skirts because they sit cross-legged while shooting. I didn't know this either.

But a few of the good Samaritans, again, leant me something to sit on and helped me navigate my camera settings.

I don't think I shot a single printable photograph the first 30 minutes of the game. So for the final 10 minutes I decided to just sit on my bucket and watch.

It was a completely different view.

I didn't have to tweet. I didn't have to take notes. I had given up on the photos. So I just watched the players, the coaches, the game, the story unfold.

I was on the baseline, 10 feet from John Beilein and his bench. I heard the players curse. I heard Beilein yelling about ball screens. I heard them in their huddles. I watched them watch their coach. They were these kids that I had covered all season, kids I had come to know, but in that moment they were different.

The game was happening in front of me, but my eyes were drawn to the bench, to the white board in the assistant's hand, to the way Beilein's mouth ticked when I saw how he wanted to yell at a player but chose not to. I had never taken in a game like that.

Duke was more athletic and more talented, no doubt. I think Beilein would agree. But for some reason, they couldn't come up with an answer for Michigan's balanced scoring attack. And Michigan kept coming up with defensive answers for Duke's. With six minutes remaining, the Blue Devils had a 10-point lead, but they just couldn't put their foot on Michigan's jugular. I knew the Wolverines were coming back and I had—literally—a front row seat.

So I just sat there on the baseline, forgetting about the camera in my lap.

I had grown up loving Duke basketball. I watched their women's coach, Gail Goestenkors, a Michigan native, beat Tennessee's Pat Summitt during the '99 NCAA Tournament. I had played on Duke's home court during a high school basketball tournament. I ran those rickety, wooden stairs after. Duke was *Duke*. But I knew Michigan could win this one.

With less than two minutes remaining, Tim Hardaway Jr.—then a freshman—hits two jumpers, pulling Michigan within one. Irving responds. Darius Morris nails a shot.

Nolan Smith takes a jumper and makes it. But Morris had fouled him. Smith, with the Blue Devils up two, has an and-one opportunity.

And in the most un-Duke-like way I could imagine, he misses. Zack Novak rebounds, sends it to Morris, and as they're charging down the court toward me, I remember the camera in my lap and pull it to my face and just start clicking like a madman.

Morris drives into the lane, elevates off one foot and sends a high, one-handed floater toward the hoop.

I stop clicking and watch the action unfold through the lens. I was waiting for something I had seen but more importantly—heard—before: the sound the perfect shot makes.

It happens when there's the right amount of wrist flick, extension, arc, and timing; when there's the perfect angle, the ball will hit the underside of the heel as it goes through the net. It's a ding-swish sound.

It's the sound every shooter knows. It's the sound every shooter searches for.

Morris' shot that night was the antithesis of that sound: *Ping*. Off the heel. No good.

A little more arc, it swishes. A little less arc, it goes in off the glass.

But it hits the heel. Michigan loses.

Morris collapsed to the ground in front of me. I continued taking photos.

Not until later did I consider how sterile this all was. Here, Morris—at his most vulnerable, missing a shot like he did, on the stage that he stood on—had collapsed into his raw emotions.

Photo by Chantel Jennings.

And me, thinking as a journalist—not as someone who was once trusted to take that last-second shot, someone who has both made and missed that last-second shot—took photos of his pain, sprawled there on the floor.

For so much of the season, I had related to the players as people, as I think all good journalists do. But my connection was different from every other journalist on the beat. We had mutual friends. I would see players at parties and on campus. I was in a 24-person class that semester with eight guys on the team. We were peers in a way that will never be true again in my professional life. It changed the way I covered the team, changed the way I saw them, changed the way I will forever relate to college athletes.

But in that moment, Morris was not my fellow student. He was my photo.

He left the court. I walked to the post-game press conference. Questions and answers. Some sadness, but the emotion was all contained.

From there we went to the locker room where for the first time since that photo, I realized what had *really* happened. The season was over. This team would never play together again. To stand in front of players whose futures depended on these games, to see the emptiness and frustration up close, was jarring. It was as though a tornado had gone through the locker room. Players stood around looking at the ground, saying little. Some were crying. Some were in shock.

Years of preparation had gone into each player's development; months of preparation had gone into this team. And in one instant, that was completely over.

So yes, there was the game and *that* was my story. But that game, not just Duke-Michigan, but basketball as a whole, had become these players' lives, and that too was my story.

Zack Novak stood closest to the door, and in a scrum of the media he silently made an analogy to how he felt like he was at a funeral, and I remember thinking how perfect it was.

Certainly there was something to celebrate, but the only reason they were raising that point now was because it was all over. The season had died with a single missed shot. Did you now mourn? Or celebrate? And when you need to do both, how do you balance those two?

I walked out of the locker room and to my computer on press row where I began transcribing. Minutes later, Morris emerged onto the court, shuffling to the place where he missed that shot, just feet from where I had been sitting with my camera, and shot an invisible ball into the hoop.

This time it went in, right? Because it's always that easy.

And that's why I love sports—it's one of the few places where really anyone can win, anyone can lose.

Sports push the threshold of the question that's hard for all of us to answer: what if?

What if Morris had stayed after practice that one day and worked on one-handed floaters in the lane? What if he had passed instead of shot? What if I hadn't joined the *Daily*? What if I had never discovered this passion?

What if?

The hardships and struggles, the wins and losses of sports are the greatest analogy we have for life. Sportswriting is the only self-help writing that the majority of the population will ever read. And that means something.

No matter how many times people avoid thinking about losing their spouse or parent or child, they'll read a sports story about an athlete going through the same tragedy, and their heart will hurt and maybe mend a little. No matter how many times people avoid thinking about sickness, they'll relate when an athlete opens up about how cancer affected him. Or how it didn't. Or how it will.

Our words can be about Duke and Michigan, about point guards and centers, but at our best, when that moment strikes, we're writing about life.

That's what I really learned in Time Warner Cable Arena. And for that, I have Beilein and Morris and that entire Michigan basketball team to thank. I don't know if I ever told them that.

We left that Sunday around 4 p.m. and arrived in Ann Arbor well after 1 a.m. State troopers pulled us over twice—the other beat writer got a ticket in West Virginia, I got one in Ohio. I laughed. It seemed right. It was a *Daily* road trip after all.

When we walked into the *Daily* newsroom each section was working to hit our 2 a.m. deadline. The editor-in-chief walked up to me and gave me a hug. The photo editor did the same and said my picture of Morris was perfect.

It was. But it was also sad. And I was OK with both of those facts.

The managing sports editor gave me a hug and asked how the trip was.

I didn't say that it was crazy or fun or miserable (truthfully, it had been all three).

I told him I had decided that this is what I wanted to do for the rest of my life.

It was an insane trip—20 hours in a car over an 85-hour period, seven stories, countless photos, four speeding tickets. I was beyond exhausted. My intake of Coca-Cola and coffee doubled my intake of food over the previous three days. I can't remember whether I had showered or not.

But I was boundlessly happy. And I knew my editor and so many other people in that newsroom knew exactly how I felt. They had been there. They had felt that.

And I knew no matter how many times I would try to explain that feeling to my friends or my family, the only people who really got it were the other sportswriters who had attempted something equally "stupid" (which journalism was, after all, right?).

That night while laying out the sports pages in my delusional, sleep-deprived state, I was so happy.

I was happier than I was at the St. Patrick's Day party, happier than I was in my English classes, happier than I was nearly anywhere. And I knew that if I could be in a community with other writers where I felt that happy, that liberated, that insanely satisfied even once in a while, I wanted to do this forever.

Chantel Jennings worked as a *Daily* sportswriter and editor from 2008 until graduating in 2011. However, not even graduation could keep her away from the place that shaped her career. She edited and helped to publish the *Daily*'s first book, *Michigan Football: A History of the Nation's Winningest Program*, in 2011. Following graduation, she worked for ESPN.com, covering Michigan as a beat reporter before moving to Portland in 2014 to cover the Pac-12 for ESPN.com.

SEARCHING FOR REACTIONS

CHRIS DZOMBAK

May 1, 2011

May 1, 2011 was a Sunday. I'd just arrived back in Ann Arbor from a weekend trip to Chicago, where I was shooting the premiere of a musical written by recent Michigan graduates. I had just started to edit my photos from the weekend when news broke that American forces had located and killed Osama bin Laden in Pakistan.

I think I first heard the news break on Twitter. I was tired after five hours on a train, but I decided to grab my camera and bike around campus. I hoped I could find some photo-worthy reactions to what would surely be a defining moment in history.

I thought finding students celebrating would be easy. Students tend to react openly and visibly to major events—a huge rally spontaneously formed at the center of campus when Barack Obama was elected president in 2008—but the campus was relatively empty. Final exams had ended a few days before.

I found one guy, a recent Michigan graduate in public policy, skateboarding and chanting "U.S.A! U.S.A!" I shot a few frames from the sidewalk as he turned the corner from Church Street onto South University Avenue. Those photos were blurry and unusable, except for one: It captured him looking straight into my camera, with the American flag rippling in the night air over his head. As he continued down the street, I biked after him to get his name for the photo's caption.

I ventured further into the neighborhood south of campus, and I found a group of recent graduates on their porch singing along to some patriotic country song. One was wearing an American flag as a cape. I

Photo by Chris Dzombak.

shot a few photos, but the skateboarder was by far my best photo from the night. Another 10 minutes of searching didn't yield any more photo opportunities, and I headed back home to send my photos to the newsroom in time for deadline.

The photo ran online with a story titled "Campus Reacts to Killing of al-Qaida Leader" for the *Daily*'s summer edition and was also picked up by The Huffington Post.

Working for the *Daily* was a great experience because of the range of subjects I got to photograph; everything from breaking news to student musicals presents its own challenges and rewards. But this photo will remain, alongside some of my photos from Election Day 2008, as one of the most significant moments I've had the responsibility—and honor—to document.

Chris Dzombak was a photographer and assistant photo editor at the *Michigan Daily* from 2008 to 2012. After graduation he spent a year in New York helping to build the NYT Now iPhone app for the *New York Times*. He's currently an iOS developer at the *Times* and living in Ann Arbor, where he still enjoys biking around town.

THE MAN IN THE MIDDLE, AND A ROOKIE REPORTER'S MISSTEPS

STEPHEN J. NESBITT

October 28, 2011

I was awaiting an elevator in the belly of the Mercedes-Benz Superdome in New Orleans moments before Michigan and Virginia Tech kicked off the 2012 Sugar Bowl when my phone buzzed with a text message from a *Daily* colleague.

"You did it better, man," the message read.

Confused, I pulled up Twitter and found a flurry of notifications that, once pieced together, explained that ESPN had just aired an emotional profile of Michigan senior center David Molk, who lost his mother to cancer in the seventh grade. I knew the story well, as I had written a 2,500-word feature on Molk and his family two months earlier.

Back in the Superdome press box, I pulled up the video and watched a near carbon copy of my opening and closing scenes play out on my computer screen, narrated by ESPN video feature king Tom Rinaldi.

Now, I didn't really do it better. I just did it first.

My initial reactions were pretty scattered. I was proud I had uncovered a story worth telling—and retelling; I was surprised ESPN had never contacted me about the story; mostly, I was astonished the Molk family was ever willing to share their story on a national broadcast.

That brings us to the story behind this story.

Before we dive into the skinny of how it all came together, understand this: If you're looking for an immaculately reported profile that pulled all the right strings, this isn't it. If you'd like to read about grave reporting missteps and how I broke a cardinal rule of journalism, though, proceed at your own peril.

It was early October 2011, and I was desperate. I had three weeks to find, report, and write a feature story for the *Daily*'s Football Saturday section that would be circulated around campus and around Michigan Stadium when the Wolverines tangled with Purdue.

After a few fruitless days of mining for longform story ideas, I settled on a simple pitch: David Molk and defensive end Ryan Van Bergen were fifth-year seniors and longtime roommates. They had been with the team through two coaching changes and system changes—from Lloyd Carr to Rich Rodriguez, and from Rodriguez to Brady Hoke.

There was bound to be a few good anecdotes out there about Molk and Van Bergen, so I reached out to their families to set up interviews. Molk's father, Tom, responded immediately and was happy to help.

Two days later, I was on the road to Molk's hometown of Lemont, Illinois. The timing of the trip aligned perfectly. I would take in the Lemont High School varsity football team's home game that Friday night, spend the night in Chicago, and cover Michigan's game at Northwestern the next day.

I interviewed Tom and two Lemont coaches in the weight room where David spent myriad hours during high school. It was a largely routine but informative session.

What caught my ear, and where the story turned, was when Tom Molk mentioned, offhand, that perhaps his son's innate aggression came from "when he lost his mother at age 12."

I didn't ask Tom the obvious follow-up question—what do you mean by "lost?"—because it didn't seem like the right setting, with two hulking coaches sitting beside him. Tom is an imposing man himself, standing all of 6-foot-5, so I opted to tiptoe around the comment and come back to it later.

After the interview, I stepped outside and did a quick Google search for "David Molk mother" but found nothing. Tom had already hurried back to work, so I decided to ask around at the Lemont football game that night.

As darkness crept over the complex, the Lemont athletic director walked me through the concessions tent. In the back, a few men stood over grills preparing a piping-hot array of barbeque specials.

One man introduced himself as John Buttney. Once I explained why I was in town, his eyes lit up. His son had played high school football with David, he said, and would be at the game later that night.

We spoke for a few minutes, and I asked John if he knew whether David's mother was in the picture.

"She died, I know," he said, shaking his head. "It was cancer, I think, but you should ask my boy. He should know."

John called me back a few hours later and introduced me to his son, Ryan, and two other former teammates, Nick Palermo and Sean Brickey. The trio shared story after story with riotous laughter, and I eventually circled around to ask if any of them knew about David's mother.

Palermo nodded and started into a story cemented into his mind.

It was the last game of the seventh-grade season, he said, and David's mother, Gail, was watching from the grassy hill beside the field. Her cancer had spread to her brain, and it was clear this would be the last game she'd see him play. Late in the game with his team near the goal line, the coach motioned for David, an offensive lineman, to move to running back.

On his third try, David plowed into the end zone and kept running. He ran out the gate and up the hill and handed the ball to his mother.

The four of us were all holding back tears by the time Palermo finished the story, and it was pretty clear where my story needed to begin.

Over Michigan's bye week, I sat down with David Molk and Ryan Van Bergen, the subjects of the initial story pitch. They were wildly entertaining, recalling one remarkable story after another—most of them nowhere near fit for print.

Eventually, Ryan took off to see the trainer, and the mood softened. I asked David if he'd be willing to talk for a few minutes about his mother. He was surprised, clearly, but quickly agreed.

I told him about the story Nick Palermo, his former offensive line partner, had shared, and David confirmed it. His voice was shaky, but he recounted the scene in wonderful detail.

"It's kind of something I've never told anyone before," he said. The toughest, meanest man on the Michigan football team wiped tears from his eyes. "I got my heart from her," he said. "No doubt about it."

A few days later, I had what I felt was close to a finished product. David and I tried to find a time to meet up to look over the details, but with two days left before deadline, nothing seemed to work out. So, naturally, I just dropped the file in his email inbox with instructions to verify the details—names, dates, et cetera.

Now, when you're dealing with such a sensitive topic, you don't want to screw up the details. That was my mental justification. But sending your copy to a subject is, for any journalist, a critical mistake.

There were plenty of other ways to verify details, of course, but at 20 years old I decided this would work out just fine. And it did, at first. David replied later that afternoon with a few quick fixes and wrote, "I'm glad I agreed to this story. More importantly, I waited for the right reporter."

Not five minutes later, another email dropped into my inbox. It was from his father, Tom. "Hold the presses!" he wrote. "Not approved!"

David called a few moments later and said the story couldn't run, per his father's directive. It was too personal, too detailed, and too sensitive.

It was only then that I realized I had neglected to tell Tom the direction the story had turned—another journalistic error. And, evidently, David hadn't told him either.

If the family didn't want it written, I certainly didn't intend to publish such a sensitive story. But since David had been so honest and so earnest about having the story center on his relationship with his mother, I never expected any resistance.

With deadline leaving precious little time to reboot the story, I drove to David's apartment to discuss our options. We called Tom, who said, in short, "The first page and the last page have to go." Those pages detailed the scene at the seventh-grade football game.

"It's too personal," Tom said. "One day you can write David's biography, but you can't print this now."

When he hung up, I told David there was no way I could simply axe the opening and closing scenes—they were the crux of everything else in the story. He agreed. He didn't want it to go, either, so we instead softened some of the language.

It was past midnight by the time I left his apartment and hurried back to the newsroom. Relieved, I explained the situation to my editors and settled in to finalize the story with only a few hours to spare.

I returned to the *Daily* by 7 a.m. that Friday morning to pick up a few fresh copies of the newspaper. I pulled out the Football Saturday insert and rifled through the pages to find the feature.

There it was in the centerfold.

My phone then started ringing, flashing a 630 area code. I didn't know the number, and I was barely awake, so I let it go to voicemail. It's probably a good thing, too.

It was a call from Tom, and from his 35-second message it was clear he was, well, quite upset with me. Evidently, David had never relayed to him that he wanted the full story to run, so to Tom, it appeared I had simply ignored his requests two days earlier.

I sent the voicemail to editor-in-chief Stephanie Steinberg and managing editor Nick Spar, who advised me not to respond but instead have David explain things to his father, who would be coming into town the next day for the game.

At noon, Tom sent my editors an email apologizing for his "horrible" voicemail message and detailing the reasons for his rage. Some I understood, others I didn't. He said I had been instructed to not use David's mother's name or mention his older brother, Steve—both requests I had never heard or agreed to.

"There is nothing I can do about it now," he wrote. "The damage is done. Your paper got the scoop. Congratulations . . . the article is out and around the world. I don't have a legal leg to stand on because Dave is an adult and you had his approval.

"I can thank you for one thing! Dave and I learned a valuable lesson. The press doesn't care about the subject! The press doesn't care about any of the people mentioned! All the press wants to do is get the story and fill the page. I'm sure Mr. Nesbitt and his co-workers were high fiving in the office on this personal and extremely private information on a Michigan football player whom was a mystery until now."

That hurt, obviously. That whole day hurt until another email from Tom arrived just after 6 p.m., a touching, 180-degree turnaround that caught us all quite off-guard.

> Stephanie,
>   I've come to the conclusion today.
>   The problem wasn't the story.
>   The problem wasn't the content.
>   The problem wasn't the reporter.
>   The problem was! ME.
>   I love my wife in a way I'll never experience again. I am still trying to keep her for myself. I have a problem with sharing her to the world. This is my wife and my sons' mom and thank you for telling Dave's story.
>   I wish I could play in tomorrow's game. I think I need to vent the way Dave does.
>
> Go Blue!
> Tom Molk

The following evening, after Michigan dismantled Purdue, 36–14, Tom Molk sent another message. He had been overwhelmed with positive responses from family, friends, and customers, he said. "Would it be too much to ask you to send me 10 copies?"

We were more than happy to.

Two months later, the Molk family told its story, proudly, for a national audience.

Stephen J. Nesbitt was a reporter and sports editor at the *Michigan Daily* from 2009 to 2013. In 2012, he won the Big Ten's William R. Reed Award. During college he freelanced for the *New York Times* and *USA Today* and interned at the *Pittsburgh Post-Gazette* and the *Indianapolis Star*. He returned to the *Post-Gazette* after graduation to cover West Virginia University's football team. He currently covers the Pittsburgh Pirates.

40 YEARS AFTER LENNON CAME TO TOWN

JOSEPH LICHTERMAN

December 5, 2011

I was one of the youngest people in the room when I first met John Sinclair at the Ann Arbor Public Library. It was December 2011, and Sinclair was in town for a whirlwind weekend commemorating the 40th anniversary of the John Sinclair Freedom Rally.

On December 10, 1971, thousands packed Crisler Arena for a concert featuring an unbelievably star-studded lineup to rally for Sinclair's release from prison. He had been convicted more than two years earlier after he sold an undercover police officer two joints.

The panel discussion that Friday night at the library was set to kick off the weekend of celebrations and an exhibit commemorating Sinclair's time in Ann Arbor. I was writing a feature on the concert's 40th anniversary for *The Statement*, the *Daily's* weekly news magazine, and I had planned to interview Sinclair the next day.

The room was packed with Townies, mostly either bald or gray-haired. Sinclair, who flew in from Amsterdam, where he now lives, was running late from the airport, so everyone mingled, biding their time until he arrived by reminiscing about the Good Ol' Days—the 1960's and 1970's when Ann Arbor was a hotbed of liberal activism.

There is no better embodiment of Ann Arbor's Good Ol' Days than Sinclair. He managed the radical band MC5, and he founded the Hill Street Commune at the corner of Hill Street and Washtenaw Avenue, which ultimately evolved into the radical White Panther Party.

But Sinclair was most famous for his arrest. He was sentenced to

10 years in prison for possessing those two joints. His arrest spurred a years-long protest movement to get him out of prison and also change the draconian marijuana laws. The concert, the John Sinclair Freedom Rally, was the climax of that effort.

But on this night four decades later, once he arrived, Sinclair, then 70 and grayed, shared the stage with a few others, including his ex-wife, who were involved in the movement. After the event, Sinclair was mobbed by well-wishers. I struggled through the crowd to try and introduce myself. As I got close, a man leaned down and in a loud whisper told Sinclair that he had stopped at a medical marijuana dispensary earlier in the day, and there was pot waiting for Sinclair—who later told me he still smoked two joints a day—at the house where he was staying for the weekend.

Not much had changed, apparently.

"Let him be, set him free"

The concert had been months in the planning, and the lineup was unlike anything Ann Arbor had ever seen or, frankly, has seen since.

Allen Ginsberg, Stevie Wonder, and Bob Seger were all on the bill. But the headliners were John Lennon and Yoko Ono. It was Lennon's first concert appearance since The Beatles had broken up the year before.

It was a coup that the organizers had managed to persuade Lennon to play at the show. Sinclair and rally organizers were friendly with Jerry Rubin, leader of the Youth International Party, the famed Yippies. Rubin knew Lennon, and he turned the former Beatle onto Sinclair's cause.

"(Lennon) just put it over the top," Sinclair told me. "All the tickets sold out in three minutes. It was the fastest selling ticket in Michigan pop music history, and that just put the focus on my case and the issue."

The crowd of 15,000 was restless by the time Lennon and Ono took the stage after 3 a.m., as the show had already been going for hours. The duo, wearing matching magenta shirts, only played a handful of songs, including one titled "John Sinclair," which Lennon wrote about Sinclair's plight.

"Won't you care for John Sinclair? In the stir for breathing air. Let him be, set him free, let him be like you and me. They gave him 10 for two," Lennon sang as Ono stood beside him playing a bongo-like drum.

The Monday after the concert, December 13, 1971, Sinclair was released from prison.

Who knows if the concert actually had any impact on his release. The day before the rally the Michigan Legislature passed a bill drastically reducing the penalties for marijuana possession—possession was now deemed a misdemeanor—and the Michigan Supreme Court then ruled that Sinclair should go free while it considered whether the state's marijuana laws were constitutional. In March, the Supreme Court ruled that the state's marijuana laws were indeed unconstitutional, and Sinclair's sentence was overturned. Michigan's new marijuana laws didn't go into effect until April 3, 1972, but on Saturday, April 1, 1972, students and demonstrators gathered in the Diag to smoke pot, give speeches, and listen to music in celebration—an event known as Ann Arbor's first Hash Bash, which has continued to occur on the first Saturday of every April.

Did it matter?

I have long had an affinity for the *Daily*'s bound volumes, and I stumbled upon a story on the Sinclair rally during one of the many times I spent flipping through the yellowing pages.

It was a cool story, a really cool story, and one I knew I wanted to re-tell. By the time I met with Sinclair that Saturday, I had already spoken to several of his associates from those days as well as historians and other experts.

I was well versed in the story, but was struggling to figure out why it mattered aside from being a storied piece of Ann Arbor's eclectic history. Had Sinclair or the concert to free him actually changed anything?

"I didn't like the way things were," Sinclair told me of his activism as I interviewed him at the Starbucks on the corner of State and East Liberty Streets. "I didn't like incipient consumer society, which you could see was going to turn into some kind of ugly, filthy thing like it is today."

After we spoke for a while, and I got what I needed for my feature, I stood up and shook hands with Sinclair. He remained seated; he said he had some work to do. As I headed toward the stairs to exit the basement of the crowded Starbucks, I saw Sinclair among a sea of college students on MacBooks, sipping lattes or mochas, and studying for their upcoming finals.

Nobody knew who he was.

And as I continued to walk away, Sinclair pulled out his own Mac and took a sip from his own Starbucks drink.

Some things, clearly, do eventually change.

Joseph Lichterman applied to join the *Michigan Daily*'s news section even before setting foot on campus his freshman year. He covered the University administration and was a senior news editor from 2009 to 2011. He served as the *Daily*'s editor-in-chief in 2012. After graduation he reported for Reuters in its Detroit bureau. He is now a staff writer for the Nieman Journalism Lab at Harvard University, where he covers innovation in journalism.

ACKNOWLEDGMENTS

Most friends and family reacted with surprise when I told them I was producing another *Michigan Daily*–themed book. The first one, *Michigan Football: A History of the Nation's Winningest Program*, took nearly two years and squashed my social life senior year. When my roommates were at South University bars, surrounded by shots and drunk students singing karaoke, I was on the second floor of 420 Maynard, surrounded by coffee, frayed *Daily* bound volumes, and three other editors singing along to 90's Pop Radio on Pandora repeat. At the time, I swore that was the first, and last, *Daily* book I'd produce. Then—not even a year after *Michigan Football* hit store shelves—I came up with the idea to compile the stories behind the stories reported by journalists whose careers began at the *Daily*. And I was back at it again.

This book would not exist without the 40 *Daily* alumni who agreed to share their side of the story or perspective from the other end of the lens. A true testament to their undying love for the *Daily*, they all jumped at the opportunity—even if they were swamped with deadlines, covering the Olympics, running newspapers and websites, or tending to their families (a few babies were born during the production of this book). I extend a sincere thank-you for carving out precious time to write your stories, dig through old files to find photos, and respond to my incessant emails.

A special thank-you to Tom Hayden for writing the foreword, testing my copy-editing skills (I will never mistake John Dewey for Thomas Dewey again), and teaching me tidbits of history.

To Scott Ham, Marcia LaBrenz, Sam Killian, and everyone at the University of Michigan Press, thank you for believing in this book and agreeing to take on the project. Because of you, important pieces of *Daily* history won't be forgotten.

I'd also like to thank the Bentley Historical Library for sharing photos and Kim Broekhuizen from the Office of Public Affairs, who helped with research.

John Bacon, President Emerita Mary Sue Coleman, and President Emeritus James Duderstadt, thank you for reviewing this collection of Michigan history. Dr. Coleman, thank you for always answering my questions when I covered the administration beat. Though I was a nervous wreck during the one-on-one talks in your office, those meetings helped build my interviewing confidence, and I couldn't be more grateful for your kindness and respect. I always appreciated that you took the *Daily* seriously and treated the staff like professionals—though I'm sure some of what we printed raised your eyebrows.

Nick Spar and Kyle Swanson each served separate terms as my managing editor when I was editor-in-chief. Though both went the law school route (perhaps I'm to blame for driving them away from journalism), they remain my best editors and supporters. Thank you both for scrutinizing every word and comma I sent and answering my frantic phone calls, texts, and emails. (I apologize for interrupting your studies.)

Chantel Jennings, thank you for letting me rope you into not just one, but two *Daily* books. I owe you a Pizza House chocolate chip strawberry milkshake. Kirk (sorry, it wouldn't be right if I used your full name), thank you for helping with photos and being my hands and eyes in Ann Arbor. Oh, and sorry you were yelled at by librarians. It's a *Daily* book rite of passage—ask Chantel.

Vanguard 2011 (Kyle, Nick, Nicole, Emily, Michelle, Nez, Tim, Sharon, Marissa, Jed, Zach, Helen, Carolyn, Josh, Eileen, and Squire), thanks for tolerating my purple ink, pink story lists, and colorful emails that were more like novels. You will always be the best group of editors I've had the honor to work with. To quote from Michael Rosenberg's story: "If you love what you do, it won't feel like work, and you will never feel overworked. It helps if you love the people who do it alongside you."

Katie Mitchell, thank you for being the only non-intimidating editor at my first mass meeting and for training me to copy edit. Those skills were invaluable for this book. Jake Smilovitz, thank you for encouraging me to run for editor-in-chief and not study abroad in Spain. You were right: I could go to Spain any day (and I finally took that trip, thanks to Meagan Choi), but leading a college newspaper was a once-in-a-lifetime experience I'll never be able to replicate.

Nikki Schueller, I might not have even joined the *Daily* if you hadn't taught me the power of journalism and what the pen can do. I owe much of my career to you.

Emily Bozek, Marie Brichta, Angela Fisher, Kendra Furry, and Amy Parlapiano, the ladies of 612 Catherine, I couldn't function without you. Amy, your late-night edits saved me, and your feedback was worth all the cheese and wine in the world. Sarah Hepner, Michelle Heller, and Caitlin Parent, thank you for always being there for me. I couldn't ask for three better friends. BPE, thanks for encouraging me to Fight Like Hell (and excusing my Monday absences) while I was EIC. Jake Serwer, thanks for being my No. 1 fan and keeping me sane during the coffee shop editing days.

Thank you to my *U.S. News & World Report* colleagues, who enthusiastically supported this endeavor, especially Consumer Advice Executive Editor Kimberly Castro; Angela Haupt; veteran author Kimberly Palmer; and Steve Sternberg, one of the greatest mentors I could ask for (I hope I always receive your emails by accident).

Mom, Dad, and Lindsay, I know you thought I was crazy when I said I was doing this again, but thank you for nonetheless supporting me every step of the way. Grandpa, I'm so thankful I received your writing genes. You're my biggest inspiration. May I only follow in your footsteps and still be writing at age 97.

Last but not least, to 420 Maynard, thank you for all the memories and for beginning my journalism career. No number of *Daily* books would be enough to repay you for the lessons learned, friendships forged, and those four unforgettable years.